Meditation for Moms

with
CD

$\mathcal{M}$editation for Moms

How to Relax Your Body, Refresh Your Mind, and Revitalize Your Spirit in $\mathcal{M}$inutes a $\mathcal{D}$ay

Kim Dwyer, *Certified PRYT Practitioner,* *and* **Susan Reynolds**

adamsmedia
Avon, Massachusetts

Published by
Adams Media, a division of F+W Media, Inc.
57 Littlefield Street, Avon, MA 02322. U.S.A.
www.adamsmedia.com

ISBN 10: 1-4405-3027-0
ISBN 13: 978-1-4405-3027-2
eISBN 10: 1-4405-3302-4
eISBN 13: 978-1-4405-3302-0

Printed in the United States of America.

10   9   8   7   6   5   4   3   2   1

Library of Congress Cataloging-in-Publication Data
is available from the publisher.

Appendix A contains text adapted and abridged from *The Everything® Guide to Meditation for Healthy Living with CD* by David B. Dillard-Wright, PhD and Ravinder Jerath, MD; copyright © 2011 by F+W Media, Inc.; ISBN 10: 1-4405-1088-1, ISBN 13: 978-1-4405-1088-5.

This publication is designed to provide accurate and authoritative information with regard to the subject matter covered. It is sold with the understanding that the publisher is not engaged in rendering legal, accounting, or other professional advice. If legal advice or other expert assistance is required, the services of a competent professional person should be sought.
        —From a *Declaration of Principles* jointly adopted by a Committee of the American Bar
Association and a Committee of Publishers and Associations

The information in this book should not be used for diagnosing or treating any health problem. Not all diet and exercise plans suit everyone. You should always consult a trained medical professional before starting a diet, taking any form of medication, or embarking on any fitness or weight-training program. The authors and publisher disclaim any liability arising directly or indirectly from the use of this book.

This book is available at quantity discounts for bulk purchases.
For information, please call 1-800-289-0963.

Contents

Introduction. ix

Part 1: Weekday Meditations 1

Chapter 1: First Things First: Meditations for Busy Mornings . . 3

Chapter 2: Midday Mindfulness. 33

Chapter 3: After School or Work 55

Chapter 4: Dinner 73

Chapter 5: Bedtime 91

Part 2: Meditations for Special Occasions 111

Chapter 6: Weekends. 113

Chapter 7: Sports and Hobbies 135

Chapter 8: On Vacation. 167

Appendix A: Getting Started with Meditation 196

Index 204

CD Contents 212

Dedication

*"And so our mothers and grandmothers have,
more often than not anonymously, handed on the
creative spark, the seed of the flower they themselves
never hoped to see—or like a sealed letter
they could not plainly read."*

—ALICE WALKER

I would like to express my deepest love and appreciation for my four children, Eileen, Erin, Joseph, and Allison. They are my greatest inspiration! KIM DWYER

I owe everything I know and enjoy about being a mother to Brooke and Brett Aved. Thank you for always illuminating my life . . . and yes, even though you're fully grown, I still love you, more than the sun, the moon, and the stars. SUSAN REYNOLDS

Introduction

> *"Hello, sun in my face.*
> *Hello, you who make the morning*
> *and spread it over the fields. . . .*
> *Watch, now, how I start the day*
> *in happiness, in kindness."*

—MARY OLIVER

Even if you have the most well-behaved children on the planet, motherhood is stressful. From breakfast to dinner to bedtime, you're on the run, dashing here and there to keep up with multiple, often conflicting, schedules and demands. Amid all this rushing about, there's little time for you to replenish your energy and nourish your spirit, which means your stress levels build.

You need a break. How to get it in the middle of your hectic day? Through meditation. But meditation offers far more than a simple break. Meditation offers unique opportunities to pause, take a breath, reconnect with your inner self or spirit, re-energize, and return to whatever is happening in your life with an open heart and a fresh attitude.

HOW TO USE THIS BOOK

To help you get that much-needed relief, refreshment, and recharge, in this book we've plotted out a day filled with typical scenarios and suggested meditations that can help you deal with those scenarios—from fussy children at the dinner table to temper tantrums at the supermarket, and everything in between. The meditations we offer vary in length and are adaptable and interchangeable, according to your needs. We offer breathing exercises as quick ways to calm situations; short and long meditations designed to help you slow down and experience what is happening within you and outside of you; prayers and mantras to soothe ruffled feathers; and yoga poses that will help you connect what's happening in your mind with what's happening in your body. Through the practice of meditation, ultimately you will achieve peaceful moments that will save the day—and your sanity.

What to Expect: Meditation

Meditation may be a foreign concept, something that other "enlightened" people do. You may think it requires a lot of time and involves a learning curve. In fact, meditation is something anyone can do, anywhere, anytime. All it requires is pausing to breathe and to quiet your mind, something anyone can learn in about thirty seconds. For the purposes of this book, meditation includes anything from simple breathing exercises, to reciting (or merely thinking of) prayers or mantras, to guided imagery, to yoga poses. It can be as simple and as pleasurable as gazing out a window and watching a bird at the feeder.

Throughout the book, we'll provide instructions that will help you with each meditation. With meditation, there is no right or wrong. When, where, how, and why are all up to you. The meditations are being offered as a way to help you with the everyday stresses of motherhood and to help you broaden "stolen minutes" into an ongoing practice, if you so choose.

Some meditations are a matter of seconds, while others can last as long as twenty minutes—and more. Our primary hope for you is that you will integrate the practice of meditation into your daily life, calming the chaos that comes with motherhood and connecting with your deepest desires. The more you meditate, the happier you—and your children—will be.

That being said, letting go of the need to plan for meditation is most important. We know how busy mothers are, so we've designed the book to help you squeeze in ten minutes (or less) here and there. We already know that those few minutes a day can lead to increased confidence, happiness, and peace. The path to being happier and feeling more fulfilled as a mother is minutes away, so we invite you to turn the page and begin our journey together.

Meditating with the CD

Oh, wait, there's a bonus! An hour of recorded meditations is included. Some are the same or similar to meditations in the book, and some are entirely new. We've created an assortment, offering you the opportunity to sample a variety and to experiment with duration, depth, and so on.

To begin, find an hour when you are able to simply relax and listen to the CD, with no agenda. Just listen. Get familiar with these simple meditations so you will know what's available to guide you on this journey. If you feel like following along with a few of them, do so. Remember, there's no right or wrong way to meditate, and these guided meditations are only tools to help you begin and deepen your practice. You may gravitate toward certain ones, using them again and again . . . or you may feel inspired to create your own CD, which is a marvelous idea.

Think of the CD as a gift you can give to yourself, when you feel out of sorts or tired. Let the soothing sounds of the guided meditations bring you to a place of quiet and peace. Who knows? Miracles could occur!

HOW TO USE THE CD

The audio CD that accompanies this book is meant to help you meditate no matter how little time you have. It includes several guided meditations as short as one minute, plus others that are five, ten, and even twenty minutes long. Use this CD at any time for a refreshing meditation break—even if you're sitting at your desk!

PART 1

WEEKDAY MEDITATIONS

It's a simple fact that moms lead very busy lives, particularly during the work week, when work schedules, school schedules, activities, and errands have to be coordinated and managed. Having more than one child adds to the stress, but even one can present ongoing challenges. Most moms want to be the best mother possible, fulfilling and surpassing their child's physical, mental, emotional, and spiritual needs. Every mom starts with good intentions . . . but life with kids is complicated—and demanding.

In this first part of the book, we'll be guiding you through a "typical" work week, addressing common problems moms face, such as getting everyone off to school, chauffeuring kids to various activities, serving nutritious meals, getting homework done on time, adhering to bedtime schedules—and enjoying your children. We've designed the book as a resource you can use when frustration peaks or energy flags; we provide everything from quick breathing exercises to twenty-minute yoga meditations that will make your everyday life flow a little more smoothly.

We'll also be encouraging you throughout to develop a meditation practice—and you really don't have to put much effort into it to make that happen. If you sample meditations as needed, on a regular basis, you'll soon adopt many of the techniques, and you may also discover the amazing benefits that come from deeper, more consistent, mindfulness meditations.

For now, let's get you through the peaks and valleys of a normal day. . . .

1

First Things First: Meditations for Busy Mornings

"There is no way to be a perfect mother, and a million ways to be a good one."

—JILL CHURCHILL

The alarm goes off, and there's no time for lolling. You have to hit the ground running. Your mornings require two cups of strong coffee—minimum. Even if you're the type of mom who lined everything up the night before, things always go awry. Someone spills all the milk before the cereal bowls are filled. Your son's favorite shirt didn't make it into the laundry, and he's refusing to wear anything else. Your daughter is badgering you for help with homework you thought she'd finished the night before. And you're worried about an appointment you can't be late for—and you need to look up one more thing online before *you* can dash out the door.

No wonder you don't leave your house feeling inspired, energized, and ready to take on the world. If you're like the vast majority of moms, your hectic mornings heap on frustration, create a sense of dread, and leave you feeling exhausted—and the day has just begun!

Wouldn't it be nice to tackle your mornings with gusto? Wouldn't it be great to confidently greet the morning and feel a surge of positive energy with every sunrise? Don't you wish you had a better way to handle the upsets? Even if you can't make every morning perfect, you *can* start feeling better about them—and feeling more empowered to handle anything the day throws at you! What you need is "me-time," at least a few minutes to gather your energy, focus your mind, and ground yourself before you take on the morning. Let's start by looking at the basics of meditation.

Why You Need Me-Time

Me-time is just that—time that belongs *solely* to you. It sounds divine, but you've likely been inundated with things to do and running on automatic pilot for so long that you can't even imagine carving out time when no one else's needs take precedence. Unfortunately, like most mothers, you've got so many things to do every day that you may swim mindlessly through the busy schedules, the piles of laundry, the cooking, the cleaning, and the mothering. The hectic pace and endless list of demands are why you don't have time to experience what it feels like to be in your body when, oddly enough, that's *exactly* what you need. Taking precious moments throughout your day to revitalize and renew will make you a happier, healthier, and more patient mom.

MEDITATION BASICS

"I love people. I love my family, my children . . . but inside myself is a place where I live all alone and that's where you renew your springs that never dry up."

—PEARL S. BUCK

In its simplest terms, meditation is a quieting of the mind, using your breath to slow things down, relax, and connect with the *you* in you (the parts of yourself that can become blurred or overrun by the demands of daily life). Some forms of meditation are called *mindfulness* meditation. To us, this means mindfully paying attention to your thought process, choosing to slow thoughts or to discard thoughts, welcoming peaceful thoughts, and paying attention to what is happening right here, right now. Often mindfulness means turning off distractions and focusing on whatever you are doing. Mindfulness can also mean choosing to do what you are doing with intention or a chosen purpose. Intentions are similar to prayers in that you are consciously choosing and holding a desire that you wish to manifest—for yourself and for others.

Breathing plays a very important role in meditation. Your breath is a marvelous tool for slowing down, quieting your mind, connecting to your body, releasing tension, and breathing in relaxation, healing, and energy. Here's what you need to know:

- When breathing during meditation, if possible, breathe in through your nose and breathe out through your nose. If it seems too stressful, breathe in and out through your mouth until you have better control of your breath.

- Most of us breathe too quickly and too shallowly. To learn to breathe more slowly, breathe in to the count of five, pulling air into your lungs and into your solar plexus, allowing your belly to swell, pause briefly, and then breathe out to the count of five, allowing all the air to slowly expel, allowing your belly to sink. Breathing in from your diaphragm (rather than your lungs) will help you learn to deepen your breathing. It helps to place a hand on your belly so you can feel it rise and fall as you draw in and expel slow, deep breaths.

- When you are seated during meditation, be sure to lengthen your spine and lift the crown of your head gently toward the ceiling while keeping your chin tilted slightly downward (to gently elongate and stretch your spine). Sometimes it helps to cross your legs and place your hands lightly on your thighs, but it is fine to sit however you feel comfortable. If you sit on the floor, placing a soft rug or pillow under your hips may feel more comfortable.

- Closing your eyes and placing your palms up may help you relax and invite spirit in. Some like to touch their index fingertips to their thumbs, but whatever feels comfortable is fine.

- Playing soft instrumental music, or soothing chants, chimes, bells, or whatever calms you, may increase your level of relaxation and deepen the experience.

- All yoga poses are physical meditations that also connect with mind and spirit. Yoga poses should never feel forced, and all are adaptable to accommodate physical limitations. Children love yoga, so it offers unique opportunities to spend time with them and to teach them something that could greatly benefit their quality of life.

No matter what you are doing, or what is going on in your life, you can *choose* to do it with your full presence, thereby performing it mindfully. You can mindfully drink your tea, take a shower, and cook your children breakfast, and all it takes is focus and intention, doing what you do moment by moment, breath by breath. Anything and everything you do mindfully become a meditation if you do it with calm and silence, breath by breath. Pausing to stretch or execute a yoga pose or even take a walk can be done as a meditation.

Meet Your Chakras

According to ancient Buddhist beliefs, chakras are wheels of energy that swirl in circles located throughout your body. The seven major chakras proceeding up your spine are: root, sexual, solar plexus, heart, throat, third eye, and crown. Because energy can stagnate in these centers, meditation and yoga often focus on releasing energy or whatever resistance may be clogging your chakras. Your root chakra is related to survival; your sexual chakra is related to sex and creativity; your solar plexus, to personal power; your throat, to expression; your third eye, to intuition; and your crown, to spirit. Many consider the heart chakra to be the most powerful chakra. Thus, many prayers and meditations speak of opening your heart center, which we will also show you how to do throughout the book.

PREPARE TO MEET YOUR MORNING HEAD-ON

"If we learn to open our hearts, anyone, including people who drive us crazy, can be our teacher."

—PEMA CHÖDRÖN

Those few precious minutes before you leap out of bed can improve your day substantially—and all you have to do is pause for five minutes to focus and gather your energy. Hopefully, you've gotten your eight hours of beauty (and brain) sleep and have awakened feeling refreshed. If so, this meditation will be icing on the cake. If you haven't gotten enough sleep—for eons—this meditation can leave you feeling refreshed and ready to tackle your morning.

Awakening Meditation

Let your day begin with a few nourishing moments by pausing to meditate. An awakening meditation is an opportunity to ground yourself and create intentions for how you want your day to go, which can positively affect the way things *do* go.

Awakening meditations don't have to be complicated or take much time—although taking time to incorporate breathing and stretching meditations is ideal. A simple breathing in and out meditation that includes positive affirmations can be an ideal way to start your day. Often, slowly breathing in and breathing out is used to mindfully integrate your affirmations.

1. Lie on your back with your arms at your sides in a relaxed manner, or, if you like, place them, palm sides down, on your stomach so you can feel your breath entering and exiting.
2. Begin by stating your intention: "Today is a new day with twenty-four new hours to live; thus I gratefully choose to begin my day with meditation."
3. Then, as you slowly inhale, breathe in this thought: *I vow to start each and every day with an open heart.*
4. Pause briefly, and then, as you slowly exhale, breathe out this thought: *I vow to accept with compassion what comes my way.*
5. Repeat this meditation four or five times.

Once you have grounded yourself and created your intentions, physical meditations in the form of yoga poses will help you integrate body, mind, and spirit, which is why we will often include yoga or yoga-like poses as a way to deepen your meditations.

Throat Chakra Meditation

The energy located in your throat chakra has to do with personal expression, which can often become blocked. Taking a moment to open it in the morning will help you express your true feelings, with full power and intention, throughout your day.

Sit on the side of your bed, inhale deeply, and as you exhale, stick out your tongue as far as you can and say "Ahhhhhh." Do this forcefully. As you stick your tongue out, notice how the sound emerges. Notice that you can choose to make your words harsh or kind. Sticking out your tongue will relax your throat and stimulate your throat chakra, reminding you about truth telling. When your heart and throat chakras are stimulated, you cannot help speaking from a place of love and compassion. Sometimes the truth hurts, so take a moment to create an intention for your day, such as "May all of the words I speak today be filled with love, compassion, and truth."

No Pain, No Gain?

Contrary to that exercising maxim "no pain, no gain," yoga poses should never feel painful. Strong sensation is okay. It's your body telling your mind that negative energy, tension, or old memories may be stored in that area. The information should be viewed as an opening to work on whatever is causing the sensation. If you feel true pain, immediately alter the pose to decrease your pain. Over time, you will be able to stretch a bit farther. The goal we suggest when using this book to create a meditation practice is to focus on the physical meditation that yoga provides, not to build muscle and strength.

LAST-RESORT MEDITATIONS

"Some days I feel like everyone in my world has plugged themselves into my kidneys. I'm so tired."

—GWYNETH PALTROW

Last-resort meditations are just that: one last attempt to get a handle on your emotions and live your life from a place of peace and strength. Last-resort meditations will be offered throughout the book so that you will have options for those times when things don't go smoothly, for those situations that don't respond to any of our other suggestions or have spiraled out of control. In those situations, you may need an overarching solution, something that will reach beyond the present situation and get you back on track in a hurry; or you may need a quickie breathing exercise that gets you back to feeling centered and ready to take on the world.

Sometimes mornings get off on the wrong foot and you really need to hit the ground running. The best way we know to do that is to regroup, more fully inhabit your body, and ramp up your energy. Hence, a few suggestions that will arm you for the day.

Ramp Up Your Energy Meditation

If you have just one minute, stand up, with your feet hip-width apart (each foot should be directly under its respective hip), knees slightly bent (also known as *soft knees* because they're not rigid or snapped to attention as they would be when standing normally).

Bring your hands onto your thighs. Inhale, and arch your back, gazing upward, sticking your buttocks out. Then, quickly exhale and round your back, tucking your tailbone and bringing your chin toward your chest. As you move, breathe in and out of your nose forcefully, executing this move quickly. You could do this seven times in just thirty seconds. For the second half of your minute, stand up tall and notice how you feel filled with energy. Breathing in, think: *I have moved my body.* Breathing out, think: *I am energized.* Repeat this several times, and then resume breathing normally.

Fish Pose

If you wake up feeling upset or angry, yoga's fish pose will help you tame your emotions, regain your center, and come from a place of love—which is naturally your intention.

Lie down on a yoga mat or a rug and straighten your legs, flexing your toes upward. Reach your arms down by your sides, and with palms upward, roll from side to side as you take hold of the fleshy part of your upper back legs. Press into your elbows to bend them and use them to lift your chest upward. Let your head drop back (notice that your heart and throat charkas are open). You may want the top of your head to touch the floor lightly. Keep your legs strong and pressing downward.

Breathe slowly and deeply through your nose. Visualize your breath going into your heart and your throat and swirling around. Stay in the pose for five breath cycles, or as long as you would like. While in the pose, consciously work on releasing emotions. Let the emotions flood outward. Let this pose be a moving meditation. Breathing in, think: *I am opening my heart.* Breathing out, think: *I am aware of my emotions.* This is called *fish pose* because it resembles a fish and because a fish is flexible and strong, capable of moving through water with ease. If you need more flexibility in your life—and who doesn't?—fish pose is a great way to start.

MINDFULLY START YOUR DAY

"We learn and grow and are transformed not so much by what we do but by why and how we do it."

—SHARON SALZBERG

Mindfulness originated with Buddhism thousands of years ago. Basically, it's a practice that fosters your ability to cultivate awareness of what's happening in the present moment, without relying on past experiences or your usual way of thinking or reacting. Mindfulness is the art of paying attention, in the present, on purpose, without judgment. It's solely about bringing full awareness to where you are—the feelings and thoughts that are happening in your life, right here, right now.

The practice of mindfulness can help you learn how to stay open and choose how your mind thinks, rather than allowing random or preconceived thoughts to control you. It's about training your mind to focus on the more positive experiences in life and how you can influence them by slowing down your habitual thought process and directing your mind to savor the small moments in life, noticing the positive aspects as opposed to the negative aspects.

Mindfulness meditation is a potent form of meditation practiced by Tibetan Buddhists, among others. When Dr. Shauna L. Shapiro, coauthor of *The Art and Science of Mindfulness*, studied the effects of mindfulness meditation on medical students, she found that the students in the meditation group were significantly less stressed than the control group and reported significantly greater levels of empathy and spirituality.

The ongoing practice of mindfulness meditation can help you deal with difficult emotions, as well as be less reactive and more fully present in general. It can help you feel more peaceful, more compassionate, and kinder—toward yourself and others.

Some of the meditations we offer in this book will be mindfulness meditations, but all forms of meditation are somewhat mindful and offer similar results. We'll also offer "Mindful Mom" sidebars throughout the book to help you discover opportunities to bring this simple practice into your daily life—so you can quickly both see and reap the many positive benefits.

Mindfully Prepare for Your Day

One can be mindful about anything, even brushing one's teeth! It's as easy as slowing down your morning routine and performing each step with intention and focus, as though every single thing you do is the most important thing you have to do in your life. If you're new to mindfulness, it helps to focus on your breath for a few minutes and use that focus to quiet your mind. Then, you gather your senses and bring your full consciousness to what you are doing. Physically slow down, paying attention to sensory input (such as the feel of your clothing as it glides over your skin, or the sound of the water running when you brush your teeth). If your mind wanders, always go back to focusing on your breath. This may feel awkward at first, but what you want to avoid is habitually (and unconsciously) rushing through these activities. As you are brushing your teeth, for example, try not to think of the next activity. Instead, bring all of your attention to what's happening in that moment: the feel of the brush as you use it to massage your gums and clean your teeth, the way your mouth feels sparkling clean after you rinse. Isn't it great that you have teeth to brush? Smile at yourself in the mirror!

Mindfulness is about staying focused on what's happening right here, right now, avoiding thoughts of the past or the future. In the preceding example, just breathing and brushing . . . breathing and brushing. It's also about savoring experiences and feeling gratitude for your blessings, which we'll discuss in greater depth in later chapters.

If you have more time, adopting a mindfulness meditation practice could totally transform your life. All you need to start are time and space. (Hint: you can find amazing resources online for guided mindfulness meditations.)

MINDFULLY MEDITATE

*"It is said that when we pray one prayer
from the depths of our heart chakra,
God has no choice but to listen."*

—GURMUKH KAUR KHALSA, MOM AND AUTHOR OF
BOUNTIFUL, BEAUTIFUL, BLISSFUL

One ideal way to meditate is to have a sacred space in your home (or office) where you can retreat from whatever is going on and find a few minutes to mindfully meditate in relative peace, quiet, and privacy.

Create a Sacred Space

While you can meditate anywhere, having a sacred space is ideal. The word *sacred* simply means it's a place where you feel comfortable reconnecting with your inner self and spirit. Ideally, it would be a place in your home that affords privacy and quiet, a place where you could keep your sacred objects, such as candles or beloved objects that represent something deeply meaningful to you.

Follow these steps to create a sacred space in your home:

- Find a space in your home where you can meditate. Where do you naturally go that feels peaceful? It can be in any room of the house, or a small space within a room. Use your intuition to choose a space that feels warm, inviting, and peaceful, and claim it as your own.

- Have a cushion or soft rug that you can comfortably sit on. If you are not comfortable sitting on the floor, a chair is fine. You may also want a yoga mat, as many of the meditations are yoga poses (combining physical, mental, and spiritual meditation).

- Create an altar where you can place objects that hold meaning for you. It can be as simple as a pretty cloth or scarf draped over a small table with a vase of flowers, a beautiful shell, a piece of your mother's jewelry, or something your children have given you. These items will help you transition from the noise and chaos that usually reign to a place of quiet and contemplation. You might want a candle and something you can play soft music on. Some like to have a watch or even a timer of some sort, if their time for meditating is truly limited. (Hint: using your cell phone alarm, set to a pleasant tone, at a super low volume may not feel as intrusive as other timers.)

If you don't have space for a sacred space, you can still meditate anywhere, even at your kitchen table, in your bed, or in your bathtub! It will be helpful if you tell your husband and children that your meditation time is sacred, which, in this case, means that you wish not to be interrupted, unless absolutely necessary.

When you sit in the same place every day in meditation, the place takes on its own energy. It will feel different from the rest of the house. Eventually the kids will begin tiptoeing around and whispering while mom is "meditating." They will know that this is your time. Or they may want to sit with you, which is fine when you feel so inclined.

Me-Time: Take a Luxurious Shower

Whether you shower before breakfast or after breakfast, taking a shower—or bath—provides a few minutes for you to focus on yourself. Choose your favorite scented soap (or bath oils or gel), shampoo, and protein treatment for your hair, and revel in bringing your attention to what's happening in the moment. For example, breathe deeply and pause to feel the soothing oil as it skims over your skin, the warmth of the water as it rushes over your body, and the soothing pulsations of the showerhead as the water warms your neck muscles. Instead of rushing, gently massage your scalp and temples as you apply the shampoo and protein treatment; massage your neck or hands; or give your feet a hard scrub. Do whatever feels like pampering, taking the time to luxuriate in each sensual moment.

READY FOR ANYTHING MEDITATION

*"Better to join in with humanity than to set
ourselves apart. Aspiring bodhisattvas train by
getting more involved, rather than more detached.
In paintings of the six realms, there's a Buddha
standing in each realm, not just in a little bubble
or looking down from above, but right in the
middles of hell and the other realms."*

—PEMA CHÖDRÖN

The first few minutes before *everyone else* gets out of bed can be perfect me-time, at least enough for you to declutter your mind with a simple, quick meditation. The idea of this meditation is "nonthinking," emptying all the thoughts that sprang to attention and started marching around your gray cells the minute you awakened (most of which probably have to do with other people and not yourself). If you take these few minutes to clear your mind, you'll have a much better chance of being able to hear the wisdom of the universe (God, your particular higher power, source of creativity, or divinity). Take at least a few minutes to simply be still and quiet your mind, and the reassurance and energy that you need will come.

Choose a place that is clean and uncluttered or, better yet, go to your sacred space. It's best not to eat anything first, as you want your body to feel comfortable, not busy digesting whatever you've grabbed on the run. Plus, meditating first will improve your digestion, and after you have centered yourself, you will more likely choose to mindfully indulge in a healthy breakfast.

1. Begin by removing your slippers or socks so your feet can breathe. Those lovely feet that take you everywhere have thousands of nerve endings. Those nerve endings stimulate energy and health within your entire body, so always give them their due by welcoming them to the meditation and giving them an opportunity to participate.

2. Sit on the floor, drawing your legs in to create a folded, cross-legged posture. If you have trouble crossing your legs in a seated position, slip a folded blanket or pillow under your hips to help support your back. If this is not comfortable, sit against a wall with your back straight and your legs extended, or sit on a chair.

3. Once you are in this position, slowly straighten your spine, raising the crown of your head toward the ceiling and tucking your chin in slightly.

4. Once your spine is lengthened, relax your shoulders by dropping them down away from your ears and slowly moving your shoulder blades backward, toward each other. Although you want this to be a relaxed posture, it may help to imagine that you are loosely folding your shoulder blades around a grapefruit or a small ball.

5. Close your eyes or just lower your gaze.

6. Relax your hands onto your knees, palms up, or, if you would like, place your hands in your lap, palms up, and then bring your thumb and first finger together to form a guyan mudra, a sacred Buddhist symbol in which the thumb represents

the soul of the universe and the finger represents your soul. Touching them together represents a union of the two energies, which helps clear your mind, improve alertness, and enhance clarity. See the sidebar "The Meaning of Mudra" in this chapter for more information.

7. Inhale slowly through your nose, and exhale slowly through your mouth. Keep breathing until you achieve a natural rhythm in which the slow intake and slow exhalation are approximately the same length.

8. Spend several minutes doing nothing except focusing on your breath. If thoughts arise, do your best to ignore them, returning your attention to your breath. If it helps, when thoughts arise (and they will), silently remind your brain that you are choosing to release all thoughts and clear your mind. Soon you'll be able to achieve this without prompts from your mind to your brain.

When you feel centered, calm, and grounded in your being, uncross your legs, bring your knees together, slowly roll on your side, wrap your arms around your legs and pull them toward you, giving yourself a hug, and then release and slowly stand. As you move into your day, use your breath as a way to bring your attention back to the feeling you experienced during the meditation, and you should be ready to handle anything life throws your way. Enjoy your day!

The Meaning of Mudra

Mudra refers to an ancient, sacred positioning of your fingers, used by Buddhists to guide the flow of energy during meditation. They believed that curling, stretching, crossing, and touching various fingers allowed you to wordlessly communicate with body and mind. Far more recently, the National Academy of Sciences found that hand gestures *can* activate the same regions of the brain as spoken or written words. The prithvi mudra, created by touching the tips of your ring fingers to the tips of your thumbs (while extending and relaxing all the other fingers) during meditation, helps promote a sense of stability and increases tolerance and patience, which can prove beneficial to stressed moms. Some consider mudras to be meditation in your hands. Worth a shot in your next stressed-out moment.

GETTING EVERYONE READY

"It's not easy being a mother. If it were easy,
fathers would do it."

—*THE GOLDEN GIRLS*

Now that you've welcomed your morning and prepared yourself to meet the day, it's time to awaken everyone else and deal with the multitude of challenges ahead. One of the first challenges that moms everywhere face is getting the kids dressed, fed, and delivered to school (or to the bus stop). Kids have their own minds, which often leads to disagreements over when to get up, what to wear, what to eat for breakfast, and more.

Why not start out with a meditation that will strengthen your stance as *warrior mom*? A warrior mom does not mean a mom prepared to fight. A warrior mom is someone who anticipates challenges and employs strategies to achieve desirable results. As a warrior mom, you are decisive, authoritative, and confident in your assessments. Your ultimate goal is to minimize conflict while allowing your children their dignity and you your authority. A great way to start is to focus your energy with hara breath.

Practice Hara Breath

Hara breath is a manner of breathing designed to relieve the body, mind, and spirit of stress and to reinforce a strong sense of self. Hara originates in the belly, which is your body's central region and the site of your soul power. Hara breath will give you an abundance of energy, speed your metabolism, and clear your mind to focus on the day ahead.

Focus on doing this by yourself, for yourself, but if your children or husband wants to join you—*and you feel so inclined*—welcome them into your circle. However, always stay focused on yourself so you can fill up what feels depleted and thus have more energy to give later.

Stand with your feet slightly more than hip-width apart, and your arms straight down by your sides. Raise your arms up and squat down forcefully as you loudly say "HA!" Inhale, straighten your legs, and as you exhale, say "HA!" with even more emphasis, emanating the sound from deep within your belly. Repeat this up-and-down motion ten times, or as many times as you would like, and then get ready to feel a burst of energy!

Mindful Mom

When you serve your children breakfast, take a moment to kneel beside each, to tousle his hair, or kiss her cheek, or simply say a heartfelt "Good morning, darling." Savor the moment, make eye contact, breathe in and out slowly, and smile. Pausing for even a single beat will help both you and your child connect. It may even become the favorite part of day for both of you. Remember, mindfulness is not about judgment or pressure; it's not one more thing you have to do. These are moments to savor simply being alive and, in this case, in relationship with your children.

CHAUFFEUR MOM

"Any mother could perform the jobs of several air traffic controllers with ease."

—LISA ALTHER

By their very nature, children are restless and impatient, particularly during car trips. And we don't mean long road trips; we mean the everyday local chauffeuring that all moms have to do. Whether you're driving them to school or to day care, or driving them home or driving them to soccer practice or to piano lessons, you need a car strategy to stay calm and focused.

Driving is one activity that requires your full attention. While driving, your eyes and ears need to be focused on what you're doing. That is, after all, crucial to keeping your children safe. However, children don't know anything about driving. All they know is that their mother is otherwise occupied and they can use the opportunity to make noise, squabble amongst themselves, or pester you with questions like "When will we get there?" or "What's taking so long?" It gets a little better as they get older, but by then they've discovered other ways to irritate you, such as turning music that you find offensive up as loud as it can go, or badgering you with what seems like an endless stream of minor complaints, or unleashing a barrage of questions that they feel they need answers to, "right now!"

In order to keep the distractions to a minimum, create the atmosphere you want before you get in the car. If you have done your morning meditations, and if you pause to breathe deeply, you'll be prepared to seize the moment and set the tone. Calmly state your expectations as you get in the car, and let your children know that you need to focus on what you're doing. If they are disruptive, instead of becoming tense and stressed over it, take a moment to breathe and calm down before restating your expectations. Use the following mindfulness and breathing techniques to keep car time conflict-free.

Take Time to Breathe

If your kids are too wound up and are disrupting the focus that you need to safely drive them, pull over to the side of the road, park your car, and take a few moments to simply breathe.

It turns out that your mother was right: Counting to ten is actually a very effective mini–meditation/breathing exercise to quell emotions and regain your center. Inhale as you count to ten, and exhale as you count from ten backward to one:

- Inhale: one, two, three, four, five, six, seven, eight, nine, ten.
- Exhale: ten, nine, eight, seven, six, five, four, three, two, one.

Repeat a few times. To calm everyone down, you can have your kids join you in the exercise. For a fun way to help resistant teens participate, have them chant the sound of "Om" with you. Inhale deeply, open your mouth wide, and as you exhale, form the short-vowel sound "Aaaaaa" (ahhhhh), and then "Oooooo" (as you begin closing your mouth), and then "Mmmmmm." The sound should be vibrating in your mouth. Maybe you can make them laugh by pointing out that they make similar sounds when they wail "Oh, mom." All they have to do is really drag it out, chanting "Oooohhh-hhhmmmmmooooommmm." Welcome their mantras, allowing each to signal a calming moment, and you'll soon be ready to hit the road again.

Good Vibrations

The sound of "Om" is a universal mantra, the most often chanted sound among all the sacred sounds on earth. For most, a full-chested and slowly delivered "Om" replicates the sound of the vibrating and pulsating universe. Many also find the sound of "Om" a comforting sound, similar to home, mom, and amen. There is no actual meaning. It is not a word; it's a sound. It can be very effective in all kinds of situations, so experiment and have fun with it! It's also a great way to end meditations or yoga sessions, helping to connect spirit with mind and body.

Ignore the Noise

If you won't be in the car long, you always have the option to simply ignore them—or at least the noise they're creating. If you're certain that no one is in danger or being tortured by an older (or younger) sibling, and you've tried everything else, blotting out the noise is a viable option. While driving, you have to keep your focus on the road ahead, so focus even harder. Find a way to drown out their squabbling with a positive mantra. A mantra is a sound or word that you say over and over to create something, usually a change or a healing. It can be anything you would like it to be. Think of a mantra as a prayer. You don't have to say it aloud, although you can go that route, as well. Here are a few mantras you could try:

- *May I have peace within my heart, peace with all of my relationships, and peace with all beings.*
- *Nothing will distract me from delivering my children safely.*
- *Love is all I need to get through my day.*
- *I hear joyful noises and feel love all around me.*

Whatever you do, make them positive mantras, as they have a way of becoming part of your reality, manifesting what you say you want. If you practice a religion, certain prayers or lines in prayers may resonate. Otherwise, spend some time creating powerful, positive mantras that you can use in trying situations—and when you're meditating.

Mantra Mojo

Pronounced as it is spelled, Om Mani Padme Hum, one of the most popular mantras in the world, is intended to create compassion. Many people will begin saying it and transition into singing it, formulating their own tune. Roughly translated, it means "When the heart and the mind get together and combine efforts, then anything is possible." So whenever you need some mantra mojo, try saying, then chanting (or singing) "Om Mani Padme Hum . . . Om Mani Padme Hum."

A science called Naad holds that the roof of your mouth has eighty-four meridian points (located along energy channels) that can be stimulated when your tongue strikes them, such as when speaking. According to Naad, the meridian points stimulate the hypothalamus gland, which stimulates the pineal gland, which stimulates the pituitary gland. The pituitary gland and the entire glandular system play a role in experiencing emotions and achieving bliss, which means that the sound of a word (and the meridian the tongue strikes while saying the word) is just as important as what the word means. Over thousands of years, yogis have created mantras designed to strike meridians that will facilitate a meditative state. Om Mani Padme Hum!

LAST-RESORT MEDITATION

"To describe my mother would be to write about a hurricane in its perfect power."

—MAYA ANGELOU

So you've tried deep breathing, mantras, hara breath, and everything in your arsenal and still you feel rattled. Time to call upon another last-resort meditation. Here's a quick, yet surprisingly effective one that can help you regroup.

Eye Cupping

As a last resort, this can be done anywhere.

Cup your hands over your eyes, enough so that you cannot see any light. Close your eyes and feel the darkness for a few slow breaths. While your hands are still cupped over your eyes, open your eyes slowly. This may feel very peaceful. Imagine that you are in the deep shade in the middle of the forest. Invite peace into your little "cupped" space. When you feel peace entering and feel reassured that you are ready to handle whatever comes, remove your hands.

CHAPTER SUMMARY

This chapter has been about navigating busy mornings by maximizing opportunities to use meditations and rituals to reduce stress. The ideal goal is for you to enjoy your mornings and make them happy, productive, and nourishing for your entire family. Here are some of the ideas we provided:

- Pause for an awakening meditation before you leap out of bed each morning.
- Maximize opportunities for me-time, such as during your shower or taking fifteen minutes for meditation.
- Take charge of your mornings by teaching yourself (and your children, if you like) hara breath.
- Take time during breakfast to savor the moment with each of your children.
- Create a strategy for peaceful car rides.
- If the children are out of control and distracting you from driving, don't be afraid to pull off the road for a breathing exercise. Being late doesn't matter as much as being safe or teaching your children to behave appropriately.
- If all else fails, practice a last-resort meditation or breathing exercise to restore your sanity and bring your focus back to you.

Your morning is off to a bright start, so get out there and conquer the world—or laundry, shopping, and errands. Don't worry; we'll be right here to guide you through the next line-up of events happening around lunchtime!

2

Midday Mindfulness

"The still lake without ripples is an image of our minds at ease, so full of unlimited friendliness for all the junk at the bottom of the lake that we don't feel the need to churn up the waters just to avoid looking at what's there."

—PEMA CHÖDRÖN

It's almost time for lunch, and you're already feeling way behind. If you're at work, you finally got your rhythm going and felt pretty confident that you could manage your to-do list—until your boss sent an e-mail asking for the report you promised to deliver an hour ago. If you're at home, the plumber hasn't shown up, which means the toilets are still clogged, and you are tied to the house until he arrives—and you haven't gotten half of the chores done that you hoped to strike off your list.

Either way, the stresses of motherhood and all the responsibilities that you face each day are mounting. You're thinking about shoveling in lunch at your desk so you can keep working, or skipping lunch altogether. So *not* a good idea: a mother needs her nourishment—and more importantly, you need a break in the action.

Whether at work or working at home, midday mindfulness can truly save a mother's sanity. That teensy little break in the action can offer some amazing opportunities to slough off the tension and anxiety (that multiplied since you got the children safely off to school) and refocus on revitalizing your body, mind, and soul. Remember: a mom who takes good care of herself is far more likely to take good care of her children. A mom who takes time to soothe her mind, replenish her energy, and regroup is also better prepared to handle challenges that the rest of the day brings. So, how do you begin? How about with a meditation that will help your body release pent-up feelings or tensions and leave you feeling refreshed?

TIME TO PERK UP!

"There is a vitality, a life force, an energy,
a quickening, that is translated through you
into action, and because there is only one of you
in all time, this expression is unique."

—MARTHA GRAHAM

Let's face it: Mornings wear us down, particularly when our schedules are packed with a long list of tasks that must be accomplished—and they're always packed with a long list because it's oh so true that a mother's work is never done. If you're feeling exhausted and need an energy booster before your lunch break, combining a yoga pose—or two—with meditation can definitely perk up your energy. Remember: yoga is a physical meditation that works its magic by incorporating breath with movements—stretching and massaging your muscles and opening chakras. Yoga meditations are great ways to release tension and re-energize your body. You can always deepen your yoga meditations by incorporating focus, intention, breath work, and affirmations, as we illustrate in the following yoga meditations.

Cobra Pose Meditation

Cobra pose is a great energizing pose for the middle of the day. The nature of the movements helps release whatever stress or fears have arisen, and restore your energy—and it can be done while lying on a yoga mat or a rug, or while standing up against a wall. All of which means: no excuses; get your cobra on!

If you do it every midday, you will feel more energy and open possibilities for the second half of the day. This pose can be an antidote for depression. It also improves the flexibility of your spine, strengthens your back, facilitates deeper breathing, and releases tension. It can also help release fear, which tends to manifest itself in the lower back and can get "stuck" there. When you do back-bending postures like this one, fear can be released. Do not do this pose if you are pregnant or if your back is causing you pain. While you are in this pose, allow any fear (past, future, or current) to surface. Take a few breaths to recognize the fear. Inhale and think: *I am aware of fear from my past and fear of the future.* Exhale and think: *I breathe out all of this fear.* Then, close this meditation by affirming: "Fear no longer serves me."

Standing Cobra

If you are choosing to do this meditative pose while standing, face the wall. Place your hands shoulder height and press them against the wall. Spread your fingers, feeling them press into the wall, and bring your elbows close to your rib cage. Slowly lean forward, until your body is pressed against the wall and your forehead is resting on the wall. When you press your forehead onto the wall you will be stimulating the third eye. Stay here for a few breaths with your eyes closed. Inhale and press firmly into your hips. Exhale, lift your heart center as though you want to press it up towards the ceiling, and arch your back, letting your head reach back, opening your throat, and lengthening from your hips all the way up the front of your body. Think about the arch being in the upper back and not the lower back. Keep your neck long and not crunched. Stay for a few breaths, and on the exhale, bring your forehead back to the wall. Do this "wall cobra" a few times. This is great for an office break.

Lying Down Cobra

If you are doing the cobra pose while lying on a yoga mat or rug, start by lying on your belly. Begin with your head turned to one side and your arms relaxed by your sides. Settle your hips by rolling slightly to your right side, rolling your left thigh inward, and then rolling slightly to the left side, rolling your right thigh inward. Pause briefly to rest.

While resting, practice pushup breath. As you inhale, allow your breath to go deep into your belly, expanding your belly until it presses into the mat. As you exhale, let your belly pull inward. Exaggerate this breath to create a feeling of the belly doing pushups. This is a good exercise to remind you to breathe deeply into your belly in all meditative situations.

Do this pushup breath for a few minutes. When you are ready, bring your forehead to the mat. The area just between your eyebrows and up about an inch is called your *third eye*, which is considered a place of intuition. As your forehead rests, consider whether or not you trust your intuition. How often have you had a feeling about something or someone, and in retrospect you were correct? Women have a strong sense of intuition, which can be stimulated by first acknowledging and then focusing, at least briefly, on your third eye during meditations.

When you are ready to move into full cobra pose, place your hands, palms down, directly under your shoulders. Your shoulders should be pressing away from your ears and down your back. Pretend you are holding a grapefruit with your shoulder blades, keeping your neck long.

With your eyes closed, "look up" to where your third eye is located. This "looking up" will stimulate your sense of intuition, thereby deepening your meditation.

Lift up from the crown of your head as you press into your palms and raise your upper body a few inches. See how this feels in your body. If you feel that you can raise yourself higher, keep slowly straightening your arms. If you are strong enough, completely straightening your arms and allowing your bones to support your upper-body weight offers an intense stretch for your back. If it feels too stressful, you can try rolling a blanket and placing it under your pelvis to cushion your pubic and hip bones. If at any time you feel a slight pinch in your lower back, bend your elbows until the pinch goes away. Remember: yoga poses should not hurt.

While your shoulders are down, notice how your heart center opens. To deepen your meditation, think of your heart as a flashlight beaming light on the wall in front of you. Imagine pressing your heart forward (more of an intention than an actual movement) to release love and light into the universe.

When you are in the full expression of the cobra pose, breathe in and out of your nose for about five breaths. As you inhale, think: *I am opening*. As you exhale, think: *I am letting go*.

If you are gasping for breath, then the stretch has become too intense, and you need to lower your body until your breath flows more easily and evenly. Holding your breath is another indication that you are too deep into the stretch. As with any yoga posture, if it is more than you can handle, you may automatically begin holding your breath. Remember: your breath should be flowing easily and naturally at all times. Pushing the stretch is not desirable; proceed at your own pace, and the more you practice these stretches, the more limber you will become.

After five breaths, lower yourself to the mat, and turn your head to one side to rest. After a moment, you may enjoy releasing any muscle tension in your lower back by slowly "windshield wiping" your feet and legs from side to side.

Before repeating the pose, while resting, come up with a mental list of things you can release to make your day run more smoothly. Is there something that you are ready to let go of, maybe a few of the items on your to-do list? Are there a few things you could say no to?

Consider these things as you go into cobra pose again. As you keep opening into the posture, see yourself rising up to possibilities and to challenges. Did you notice fearful thoughts occurring in the first effort? Were you able to release them? If not, can you do so now, using your breath and focused intention?

If cobra pose feels too intense, you may want to try sphinx pose.

Sphinx Pose Meditation

This is very similar to cobra pose and has many of the same benefits as cobra but is much gentler. Lie on your belly on a yoga mat or on a rug (or press your body against the wall). Come up on your elbows, palms down, with your fingers pressing down and pointing straight ahead. Your legs are straight behind you, and your thighs are rolled in; the fronts of your thighs are moving toward each other and the backs of your thighs are moving away from each other. Relax your buttocks and legs to open up your lower back. Feel your pelvis drop into the mat or press into the wall.

Close your eyes and take a few slow breaths. When you are done, bring your elbows out to the sides and bring your head to one side. Stay resting for a few more breaths.

TAKE A SAVASANA NAP

"Naps are nature's way of reminding you that life is nice—like a beautiful, softly swinging hammock strung between birth and infinity."

—PEGGY NOONAN

If you're able, taking a restorative nap can help you reduce stress and stay healthy and available for your family. A Savasana nap has the added benefit of reminding you to be mindful as you relax and prepare to rest.

Savasana is typically practiced at the end of a yoga session as a way to rest the muscles (and the mind!) while allowing the meditative poses just completed to work their magic, but it's also a great way to quiet your mind and body and practice a refreshing silent meditation. Savasana is actually called *corpse pose* and is done while lying flat on your back on a yoga mat or a rug. Many find it more comfortable to place a bolster, rolled towel, or pillow under their knees. A folded hand towel or a scented eye pillow placed over your closed eyes will help you relax further. Some people like to play soothing instrumental music while taking a Savasana rest.

To begin, bring your arms straight down by your sides. If you are cold, bring your arms close to your body, and if you are warm, move your hands about one foot or more away from your sides. If you wish, using a light blanket can feel comforting. The intention is not to fall asleep but to remain alert in your mind and very still in your body, which is surprisingly relaxing, particularly if you maintain the pose for a good ten minutes or slightly longer. When you feel rested (or when your music or timer cues you that the time is over), roll to your side, come up slowly, pause to take a few deep, cleansing breaths, and then open your eyes.

If you want to take a nap after spending some time in corpse pose, here's what to do:

Notice how your heart and breath slow down. Notice the noises outside of your home—maybe the wind or rain, maybe cars or trucks driving by, a neighbor's dog or children playing in the distance. Just notice and breathe, listening to the noises of life. Now bring your awareness inside the house, and notice all the interior sounds, such as the humming of a heater, the air conditioner, or maybe a fan. Listen to all of these sounds while breathing slowly and rhythmically.

Bring your awareness to the sounds of your own breath, how it sounds smooth and relaxed. Bring your awareness even deeper. Can you hear vibrations? Can you hear humming? Stay with this humming, and let it soothe you into rest.

When you are ready to end your nap, give yourself a few minutes. Deepen your breath, become aware of your surroundings, and begin to wiggle your fingers and toes. Turn your wrists and ankles in circles. Turn your head gently side to side, slowly waking up your body. After a few breaths, reach your arms overhead, inhale deeply, and say "Ahhhhh" as you exhale. Roll both of your legs to the side and slowly push up to a sitting position. When you are ready, begin the second part of your day refreshed.

Mindful Mom

As you tuck your little ones in for a nap, slow down the process so you can savor the sweetness. Gently stroke your child's cheek, run your fingers through her hair, and rub her back as you sing or hum a song. In other words, don't let such a marvelous bonding moment get swept away by a laundry list of things you want to get done. They won't be babies and toddlers for long, and one day you'll long for these precious moments. Enjoy them now! Savor them now!

DO A WALKING MEDITATION

"When you are a mother, you are never really alone in your thoughts. A mother always has to think twice, once for herself and once for her child."

—SOPHIA LOREN

Walking meditations are nothing if not blissful, particularly if you live in a beautiful area or have access to rivers or ponds or woods, and they're the *perfect* occasion to be alone in your thoughts. These meditations are all about releasing the nagging stream of thoughts clattering and clanging around in your mind, and surrendering to the simplicity and beauty around you—such as noticing the tiniest, loveliest, most serene details of a natural stream. Still, the best part about a walking meditation is that going around the block will do.

When you begin a walking meditation, pretend that you have never walked before. It helps to practice in your home with bare feet before trying one outdoors. Create a clear line to walk, maybe a hallway, some place in your home where you can walk back and forth. Begin by focusing on your posture, straightening your spine from your tailbone to the crown of your head, standing squarely over your feet and hips. Feel your feet on the floor. Pretend that your feet have never touched or felt the floor, like you're on another planet and have no idea how this "new ground" will feel. Feel every inch of your feet touching the floor . . . each of your toes, the bottoms of your feet, and your heels. Feel the texture and the coolness of the tile or wood, or the cushion of the rug. Be curious about how everything feels under your feet.

Lengthen your body up through your spine to the crown of your head. Bring your shoulders down and back to open your heart center. Your chin is slightly tucked. Pretending you are learning to walk for the first time, take small steps. Step lightly and slowly. Smile while you are walking. Realize how different it is to walk without having a place to go and how refreshing it feels to be focused solely on walking, surrendering all thought about anything other than walking. You can have a beautiful walking meditation anywhere; even prisoners learn to do walking meditations in their cramped cells. Now you are ready.

Pick a place that you would like to walk—by a stream, on a path in the woods, by a fence. You can even have a walking meditation on a busy city street, but it will be more difficult and will require more concentration. Keep in mind that you have no destination, just walking . . . that's it. Let go of any worries or concerns as you walk. Keep a smile on your face. Slow your walk to a stroll. This kind of walking is not about "power walking." Let go of any agenda about walking, and focus on noticing the beauty of your surroundings. See things as if it's the first time, as if you have been blind all of your life and now you can see. Notice all of the beauty that you see, from clouds in the sky to veins in a leaf, and really look at everything, surrendering all judgment. Let go of having to arrive anywhere and simply focus on enjoying the process of walking, surrounded by light and air and beauty.

Remember that this is a meditation, which means you want to keep returning your focus to your posture and your breath. As with any meditation, your breath should be slow, rhythmical, and drawn deeply into your belly before being fully expelled. Maybe inhale for two steps and exhale for two steps. Focus on the rhythm until it feels natural, and then bring your focus back to the beauty and the simple process of walking, affirming that you are walking all of your cares and worries away.

Walk as long as time permits, and end your walk by pausing to take a few cleansing breaths. If you like, you can bring your hands into prayer position and pause to express your gratitude for the beauty of your surroundings. Notice how peaceful and quiet your mind has become, and remember this feeling so you can tap back into it when things begin to pick up speed. Notice what thoughts are first to appear. The more you learn to quiet your mind and let go of any thinking, the more surprised you'll be when insights start popping up toward the end of your walk.

Me-Time: Take a Video Vacation

If you're at home, even if you only have twenty minutes, slide in your favorite DVD, and then sink your tired body onto some soft cushions and let the story take your mind on a lovely side trip. This might work better if it's a story you already know well, so you won't feel compelled to watch to the end. If you know and love the story, you can pick and choose the portion you watch. We're big fans of certain movies that sweep us gleefully away, but you could also watch nature videos—whatever will leave you feeling refreshed and pampered. If you're at work and can take a short break, find something on the Internet that you'd love to watch for a few minutes. Hint: it could also be an exercise video, or a yoga video, or a dance video.

HAVE A CUP OF TEA

"Each cup of tea represents an imaginary voyage."

—CATHERINE DOUZEL

In the midafternoon, take a moment to indulge in a refreshing cup of tea—and do a mindfulness meditation while you're at it.

Teatime is about using all of your senses. Use your favorite teacup or even use your good china for teatime. Why not? Pampering yourself adds to the relaxation and refreshment you derive from a mindful meditation. Pour the water into a teapot or directly into your cup. Let it sit for a few minutes. Lean over and smell the scent of the tea. Look at the color of the tea. Is it gold? Think about the color of gold. What does this bring up? Stay with positive thoughts: flecks of gold in your child's eyes, the gold of a sunset or a summer flower, a gold wedding ring, or anything that comes up.

Deeply inhale the scent of the tea and bring the cup up to your lips. Before you sip, pause to feel the warmth and breathe it in. Then, slowly sip, using your taste buds and sense of smell to focus on the tea. What flavors are present? Can you taste flowers or herbs? If it's not too hot, hold a sip of tea in your mouth for a few seconds and truly savor the subtle flavors. Use all of your senses to enjoy your tea as though it were the first cup of tea you have ever experienced.

FIND A WAY TO POWER THROUGH THE NECESSARY EVILS

"A bird doesn't sing because it has an answer,
it sings because it has a song."

—MAYA ANGELOU

We've all got tasks on our plates that we find grueling, whether mentally grueling, physically grueling, or emotionally grueling. Some resist laundry, putting it off until the last moment; some resist paying bills; some resist grocery shopping—and all have their reasons for procrastinating. Gently ask yourself if resistance is really working for you. By resisting, dreading, or procrastinating, you may actually be causing more problems, making the task even harder.

Instead, psyche yourself up for the tasks that you always put off until the last moment. Add mindfulness to your daily routine!

Turn Everyday Tasks into Mindfulness Meditations

You can do anything mindfully; you can clean a toilet mindfully! Become deliberate about the toilet. Go slowly and let the way you approach this task set the tone for the rest of the day. Choose a nicely scented and organic product. Pay attention to what you're doing, instead of trying to rush through it. Notice the judgments you make about the toilet and about cleaning it. Notice how much time is wasted thinking about what you have to do, instead of simply accepting that it must be done and attending to it. Part of a meditation practice is acceptance. As you clean, focus on making the toilet clean, and think of it as a gift to your family. Imagine them noticing how delightful it feels to have a nicely scented and fresh toilet to sit down on.

Think about all the tasks that need to be done as individual meditations. Washing dishes can be a perfect meditation. Fill up the sink with soapy water, again making sure that you buy products that are beautifully scented and perhaps organic. When you plunge your hands into the soapy water, enjoy the sensation of warmth. Then, wash each glass and dish slowly, surrendering any desire to rush the process or to focus on getting them all done. Rather, focus on just one item at a time. Appreciate your dishware as you line up each item nicely in the dish rack to air dry.

You can, with practice, make everything you do a mindful meditation, by quieting your mind, focusing solely on the task at hand, using all of your senses, and breathing evenly, calmly and slowly as you work. Enjoy the time by seeing it as a restful time, devoid of rushing or multitasking. Give yourself tranquility. For example, if the phone rings while you are doing your task, stop what you are doing, take a breath, dry your hands slowly, take another breath, and then answer the phone. Give all your attention to whoever is at the other end. When you are finished with your call, resume completing the task at hand.

With everything you do, have a childlike delight. Keep a little "Mona Lisa" smile on your face. Keep your jaw relaxed and your posture upright. Feel grateful for your blessings and for the love you express by caring for your family.

MAKE PLANS FOR LATER

"At work, you think of the children you have left at home. At home, you think of the work you've left unfinished. Such a struggle is unleashed within yourself. Your heart is rent."

—GOLDA MEIR

Anticipation is almost as much fun as the experience. Did you know that if you visualize a future event (or past event) in detail, as if it's happening in real time, your brain will believe that it's actually happening? That means that you get to enjoy the experience twice!

If you're having a rough day, taking a moment to visualize something that will happen later that you'll enjoy—such as dinner with your family, or a movie with friends, or a long-awaited vacation—can really brighten your day. Build the visualization by coming to a quiet place. Then, think about the details: Whom will you be with? Where will you be? What will you be doing? Imagine the tastes and smells and textures, the sounds and sights. If you're visualizing dinner with your family, imagine your children's faces as they tell you about the day or help you fix the meal. Feel the good feelings—*as if they are already happening*—and end your visualization by stating an intention to mindfully enjoy the upcoming experience . . . before transitioning back to your daily schedule.

WHEN THERE'S TOO MUCH TO DO

"If we fall, we don't need self-recrimination
or blame or anger—we need a reawakening of
our intention and a willingness to recommit,
to be whole-hearted once again."

—SHARON SALZBERG

Every day brings with it a big to-do list. However, on those days when "too much to do" reaches an "insanely overbooked, over-stressed, freaking-out" level, it's time to stop everything. That's right: Don't do anything. Stop all thoughts. Stop the mind chatter. What you need—to maintain sanity—is to take a breather. This mindful-ness meditation will help you stop and let go so that you're ready to tackle the insanity.

Lie down on a yoga mat or a rug. With your legs extended, take a few falling-out breaths (inhale through your nose and "Haaaa" out your mouth). Bring your knees toward your chest, and hug your knees for another few breaths. Let your arms go out to the sides, and have your feet touch the mat with your knees bent. Inhale. As you exhale, bring your knees over to the right, and look to the left. Stay in this position for a few breaths. Then inhale, and exhale as you bring your knees to the other side and look in the opposite direction.

Think of your body as a giant kitchen sponge, and visualize your-self wringing out all of your chattering thoughts. Think about each thought as if it is a leaf, and visualize all of the leaves flowing down a stream. Once you are "wrung out," you are ready to absorb quiet and peace. Twist from side to side slowly, and as you do, exhale and wring out everything. If your mind resists and you are not able to stop the mind chatter, create the intention to replace the chattering with breath. Be patient with this intention, and remain in the meditation until you feel refreshed.

LAST-RESORT MEDITATION

"White-shell-woman, she moves . . . before her all is beautiful, she moves, behind her all is beautiful, she moves."

—NAVAJO SONG

Where has your afternoon gone? The kids will be home in twenty minutes, and you are already feeling anxious. While you love to see the little darlings (or big darlings), attending to their needs takes precedence over whatever else you had in mind—and so goes your afternoon. No more me-time until the clutter, clatter, and frenzy that they bring subside.

Perhaps the best thing you can do for yourself is to burn off frustration and rev up your energy. Going outside always provides a double bonus: nature and a mini-workout. Take a bike ride, ratcheting up your speed slowly until you feel the burn. Or, how about speed-walking around three blocks before the kids come home? You could also jump on your treadmill or dash up and down stairs, but we so prefer the outdoors, weather permitting.

Sippy Straw Exercise

Here's a quickie breathing exercise that will rev up your energy.

Pretend you are breathing through a straw. Inhale little sips of breath without exhaling. Sip in as much breath as you can. Fill all four lobes of your lungs with breath, and when you cannot sip anymore, then exhale out of your mouth. When you exhale and think you are done exhaling, exhale some more. This is so very energizing and should not be done in the early evening as it will keep you awake.

Many of us are not breathing fully; we have old breath swirling in our lungs. Most of us only use about a quarter of our lung capacity. When you fully exhale, you create space to bring new and fresh breath (prana) to the lungs. This full breath will release serotonin and create a feeling of peace.

CHAPTER SUMMARY

This chapter has focused on what's happening midday, when energy flags and moms need a pick-me-up. We highly recommended nutritious lunches that include a true break in the action and a little mindful eating, along with naps or rejuvenating meditations. Here are some of the ideas we provided:

- If your energy slumps, try a cobra pose to renew your energy level; to remain open to favorable possibilities for the rest of your busy, busy day; and to lift your spirits.
- If you're too busy for cobra pose, sphinx pose is a gentle pose that will give your lower back a stretch.
- Taking a Savasana meditation can also be refreshing and may lead you blissfully into a nap.
- Walking meditations will help you release nagging thoughts and surrender to the beauty around you. Best of all, you can achieve the same effect whether you're walking around your block or on a 2-mile walk in the woods.
- Having an afternoon tea break is a fabulous way to relax and pamper stressed moms. If you turn the experience into a mindfulness meditation, you can savor every drop of tea.
- Mindfulness is a productive and fun way to power through the necessary chores.
- If you feel overwhelmed, you'll feel much better if you stop everything and clear your mind of the jumbled thoughts and worries that are weighing you down.
- As your afternoon winds down, a few breathing exercises before the kids come home can really perk you up.

So you've not only survived; you've enjoyed the middle of your day, and you're feeling refreshed and ready for the kids. Of course their re-entry brings its own set of challenges, but we're on board not only to get you through but also to make the next part of your day go as smoothly as possible.

3

After School or Work

"That said, my kids are at home right now with
my husband and I'm missing something important
at my daughter's school which makes me feel sick
inside. It's a lot of balance and a lot of really
hard decision making."

—REESE WITHERSPOON

When you picture those afternoon hours with your children, you may
wish you had the ideal version where children gleefully gobble up rai-
sins and a slice of real cheese with a wholesome whole-grain cracker,
talk to you in civilized tones about the day at school, and rush off to do
their homework without prodding or chastising. Nevertheless, as many
of us learned long ago, there is no such thing as the ideal family. Even
if they are still portrayed in sitcoms—although honestly, we can't think
of one at the moment—families where children are perfect and mothers are always gracious rarely exist in reality. But that doesn't mean this
time of day can't be less frazzled and stressed than it usually is.

RE-ENTRY

"After you have children, you enter into the unknown every day. Be like a river. Be ever present and flowing."

GURMUKH KAUR KHALSA

Whether it happens as soon as you pick the kids up from school or when you pick them up after work, all moms know a thing or two about re-entry. It's those first few minutes when everyone arrives home and all hell breaks loose. Feeling liberated, the kids are almost literally bouncing off the walls, demanding attention, food, and playtime. You, on the other hand, are balancing the desire to provide nutritious snacks that won't spoil their dinner, and provide positive attention, and fulfill homework necessities—while also enjoying your children.

So what you need is a rebalancing meditation for both you and your children, if you can charm them into participating. Try this rebalancing meditation to get everyone off on the right foot.

Rebalancing Meditation

Tree pose is perfect physically and psychologically for dealing with re-entry stresses. It helps develop balance, steadiness, and poise. Stand with your feet hip-width apart. Feel the four corners of each foot pressing evenly into the floor. (Great to do outside with bare feet, weather permitting.) Lengthen your spine, and lift the crown of your head toward the ceiling (or sky if practicing outside). Feel all of the muscles wrapping around your legs. In other words, gently engage your leg muscles, especially lifting the quad muscles; lift your pelvic floor by pulling up the muscles as though you were trying not to pee and engage your abdomen by pulling the stomach muscles inward.

Bring the sole of your right foot to the inner thigh of your supporting leg (your left leg), and open your knee out to the side. (Feel free to touch a chair or counter to help with balance.)

Bring your hands together in a prayer position. Look at something that is not moving to help with balance, and focus on your breath until you feel steady. When you feel steady, bring your hands up as though you were extending your branches. While in tree pose, think about what tree you resonate with today. Are you a willow tree, swaying back and forth, or are you an oak tree, standing firm and strong? How about a cherry or apple tree? Young kids love this pose.

If you are not able to balance today, use this as an opportunity to reflect on what may be out of balance in your life. As you do balancing postures, you may notice that some days you can balance for quite a while and other days not so much. Being mindful is noticing (without judgment) the differences from day to day.

Mindful Mom

An important part of rebalancing after school or work is to truly connect with your kids. Once you are all safely home, convene everyone in the kitchen for a little chat before they dash off to do whatever it is they have to do. Ask your children how the day was, look into their eyes, listen to their responses, and spark a conversation that they enjoy. A soft touch on their arms or a warm embrace intensifies the connection. Note: you don't need food to connect, but if you choose in these moments to offer a glass of milk or juice and a healthy snack, eventually they'll connect healthy food with happy memories.

Spiritual Development

One way to reconnect with each other during re-entry is to practice something that involves spiritual as well as physical conditioning, such as yoga or tai chi. Spiritual practices typically involve discipline and learning to honor your spiritual self, which are skills you'd want your children to learn. You can practice yoga if you are healthy or unhealthy, strong or weak. Anyone at any age can begin a yoga practice. There is a teacher available for any level of student. Yoga is completely universal and can be enjoyed by anyone! Yoga uses our bodies as a kind of doorway where we can take residence in ourselves.

Yoga means *union*, union of the bodies. We have a physical, emotional, mental, and spiritual body. In our culture, we go to church or pray with our spiritual body, work out with our physical body, study with our mental body, and go to a therapist with our emotional body. Yoga brings all of the bodies together, which facilitates acceptance. The purpose of yoga is to attain happiness, peace, and ultimately bliss. Using yoga postures and breathing, we can bring balance to all of the systems of the body. It also encourages concentration, patience, self-acceptance, and inner stillness. When we find inner stillness, we are able to hear what God (or whatever we may call "our higher power") is saying to us. In the stillness, we find our spiritual body.

Finding Stillness

Sitting in stillness is what meditation is all about. A meditation practice can be very challenging. It is hard to sit in stillness. Our minds are chattering about all kinds of things. This happens to every one of us. This chattering mind is called Monkey Mind. Like a monkey that jumps from branch to branch, our minds can seem to jump from thought to thought.

Ideally, meditation should be done every day during a time that is set aside for that reason. This can be very difficult for busy moms, but you can find times throughout the day to quiet your thoughts, and the possibilities are endless as far as breath (pranayama) and yoga postures (asanas).

If you make it engaging, kids naturally love learning about practices like yoga or tai chi. They'll love proving that they can twist themselves into pretzels or hold a pose longer than you—and everyone will benefit.

Yoga Meditations Your Kids Will Love

Set aside a time for "playing yoga." Create literal and mental space for this playtime. It is nice to use aromatherapy or candles to set the tone, and you could encourage the kids to find a rock or seashell to create an altar, which they'll love and understand when you explain why an altar adds to the spiritual experience. Or simply hang a yoga poster to designate the space as a special place. Creating a sacred space is not necessary, but it can deepen the meditations.

Crane Pose with Goldfish

Crane pose with goldfish is a balancing posture that kids just love. Use goldfish crackers for this activity (there's an organic whole-wheat version, if you prefer). Stand on a yoga mat or a rug and place a few goldfish towards one end of each mat or rug. (Kids love to have their own mat to use.) Stand in mountain pose. In mountain pose, your feet are hip-width apart, with toes facing forward. Bring your arms to your sides. Allow your tailbone to reach downward, and lengthen your spine upward. Press out through the crown of your head.

Now you are ready to begin the crane pose, which you will describe and model for your children. Reach your right arm up over your head and make a crane beak with your fingers and thumb. Press your four fingers together for the upper part of the "beak"; your thumb is the bottom of the "beak." You can even draw little crane eyes on everyone's knuckles with a makeup pencil.

Bring your left foot to your left hand behind you, so that you are balancing on your right leg. When you feel balanced, your crane face can look for the fish and decide to go fishing for a snack. Try to fold at the hip as you reach down to see if your crane can pick up the fish without letting go of your left foot. Go slowly and steadily. When you have the fish in your beak, come back up while still balancing. It's fun to pretend the crane is eating, and it is even more fun to pop the fish into your own mouth. This is challenging and a lot of fun.

With children, it is important to let them play with this. They will pick up posture and alignment in time. As the mom, try to maintain your alignment so they can see how it looks. Kids will usually fall a lot, which becomes part of the play. Kids learn through play. Have the kids take turns and cheer for each other. It is normal if children want to be competitive, and it's part of our culture. If they become overly competitive, use this as a learning opportunity and talk together about how it feels. Help them to notice that competition is just one way to be, and explore together some other ways, encouraging each child's own ability. Talk about how it feels when everyone is cheering for you, and how nice it would make others feel if you cheered for them.

Animal Yoga

Pretend to be animals. Start with downward-facing dog pose: Come to your hands and knees on a rug or yoga mat. Curl your toes under, spread your fingers wide, and press your hips upward. Press into your hands as though you were pushing yourself away from the top of the mat. Pull your shoulder blades down, straighten your legs, and press your heals downward. With children, it is more about having fun than specific alignment. As they get older, instruction becomes more important.

Cat and dog stretch is another fun yoga posture for kids. Encourage the kids to make their own cat and dog sounds. Let them decide what kind of cat or dog they want to be.

Come to your hands and knees. Make sure your hands are under your shoulders and your knees are under your hips. Inhale as you lift your tailbone and the crown of your head, looking upward. Let your lower back arch downward. Pretend that your heart is a flashlight beaming light directly in front of you. When you exhale, tuck your tailbone under, round your spine upward, and lower your head. Do one execution while pretending that you are an angry Halloween cat. Go back and forth between dog and cat, and make sure you connect your breath to the movement.

Me-Time: Do Something You Love

How about creating a ritual that nourishes you that you do every day, even if five minutes is all you can find? It could be pruning flowers in your garden, enjoying a glass of lemonade while sitting in your backyard, going online to find a recipe you're dying to try, or calling your mother, best friend, or husband. Maybe you can find a quiet nook where you can light a candle and sit to write in your journal. Or maybe you'd prefer blasting a song from when you were in high school, and dancing like a maniac. It could be absolutely anything that pleases you, as long as it reminds you that you need a little pampering, too.

STEALING TIME TO CATCH YOUR BREATH

"If you find it in your heart to care for somebody else, you will have succeeded."

—MAYA ANGELOU

Once you have the kids settled, it's time for you to sneak off for a refreshing moment alone. After all, you'll need strength for the coming squabbles that often erupt—even in the most peaceful of households—when children are fussy about what's being served for dinner or over-tired yet resistant when it comes to settling down for bed.

Try this creative mothering visualization to help feel centered and grounded. Write or think of an affirming statement, something like *I see myself creatively parenting my children to the best of my ability, offering guidance and love and patiently accepting whatever crosses my path.* Relax with a few deep breaths. Feel the tension of the afternoon melt away like an ice cube in the sun. Feel yourself fill with an abundance of love and acceptance.

Visualize an area of parenting that you feel insecure with. Visualize warm sun rays shining on the parts of your parenting that you are feeling in need of strengthening. Perhaps you desire more patience, for example. Let the rays of sun turn into a giant ball of healing energy, and imagine this energy surrounding you. Allow any thoughts, fears, and emotions to rise up. Don't be afraid of them. Let them rise up, look at them with compassion, and then let them float away down an imaginary stream. Take another few breaths, and feel the lightness of letting go.

Continue your day feeling renewed and confident.

HOMEWORK HUSTLE

"My mother used to say, 'He who angers you, conquers you!' But my mother was a saint."

—ELIZABETH KENNY

There's no way around it: Most children don't like doing homework. It's hard to blame them when they've spent the bulk of the day in school. Nevertheless, to succeed in school, your children need to make homework a priority.

A little strategizing is in order. Think of ways you can inspire your children to get their homework out of the way without sacrificing the quality of their work. Hopefully the creative mothering visualization just presented will help you gather your wits, but if not, always take a few minutes to center and focus yourself before enforcing your homework rules. If you're feeling overwhelmed or bogged down by too many things on your mind, your children will sense it and rush in to create just enough confusion to breach the homework rules. Getting upset, delivering ultimatums, and arguing are counterproductive and tend to distance and frustrate everyone. What you want is harmony, and it's not always easy to achieve.

Approach the homework skirmishes as if you are your children's fearless leader—because, well, you are! Have each child write a list of what he or she has to have done by the next day and within the week. This way you can help them create an action plan—the fastest, most efficient, and best way to get their homework done—and impress their teacher. You can post a calendar on the refrigerator, or use whatever organizational tools you prefer. The goal is to do good work, efficiently. Helping them learn to create a to-do list and to focus are invaluable skills. Try this focusing exercise:

Come to your mountain pose. (See the section called "Crane Pose with Goldfish" earlier in this chapter.) To come into mountain, stand with your feet hip-width distance apart, lengthen your tail bone, and press into your feet to lengthen your spine all the way to the crown of your head.

Once in mountain pose, bring your right knee up toward your torso, and hold your knee with both of your hands. It helps to look at something that is not moving. Stay for a few breaths and then switch sides. As you concentrate on balancing, you may find that you become calmer and more energized. The next time you draw your leg up, incorporate the ujjayi breath.

The ocean-sounding breath (ujjayi breath) will calm your mind, helping you to notice what kind of thought-chattering is going on in your mind and thereby increase concentration. This breath sounds like the ocean or like Darth Vader from *Star Wars*—almost like the sound you make before you start to snore. Think about the way you fog a mirror with your breath. You make a "Haaa" sound to create the breath that will steam the mirror. This is the sound you want.

As you inhale through your mouth, slightly constrict the back of your throat. Then make the "Haaa" sound as you exhale. Now close your mouth and try to make the same "Haaa" sound as you inhale, remembering that it will sound like the sound you make before you start to snore. You want the same sound with both the inhale and exhale. This takes some practice for adults, but kids usually pick it up more easily. If you want to create more focus with this breath, hold a few seconds after the inhalation and after the exhalation.

LAST-RESORT MEDITATION

"Love begins at home, and it is not how much we do . . . but how much love we put in that action."

MOTHER TERESA

If it's not going well, and you feel yourself moments away from blowing a gasket, you need a time-out to calm the homework hurricane building inside.

Forward-bending postures will calm the nervous system. Try this short, simple exercise:

Stand in your mountain pose with your feet hip-width apart (see the section called "Crane Pose with Goldfish" earlier in this chapter). Soften your knees so they are slightly bent. Reach your arms up above your head, inhale, and as you exhale, fold over to touch your toes or reach close to them. Hang like a rag doll. Your head should not have any tension. Stay for a few breaths. You can sway back and forth, sweeping your fingertips side to side. Come up slowly, rolling one vertebra over the other like you are stacking coins. Your head should come up last. You can do this as many times as you would like, to feel calm and refreshed.

EXTRACURRICULAR OBSTACLES

"If you bungle raising your children, I don't think whatever else you do well matters very much."

—JACQUELINE KENNEDY ONASSIS

If you're a busy, active mom, it's highly likely that you're raising busy, active kids. So that means they probably have at least one extracurricular activity, ranging from piano lessons to karate or from glee club to hockey. You're either driving them yourself or organizing car pools. Either way, you'll often end up sitting in your car while they complete a half-hour lesson or watching from the sidelines as they practice soccer—and then you're waiting while they rehearse for the local theatre production or while they play in baseball, football, soccer, or hockey games. You get the idea: There's a whole lot of time you have to spend chauffeuring, waiting, and watching from the sidelines. We say maximize this time by stealing moments to rejuvenate yourself using some of the yoga poses or meditations we've described. Or, try this one: Find a comfortable place to sit. Close your eyes, if that feels comfortable to you, or just lower your gaze. Notice whatever is present in that moment, any sensations, thoughts, or feelings.

Reflect on your current life situations. Notice what seems to be your most significant challenge right now.

If your eyes are not closed, close them now. With your eyes closed, look up to the place between and above your eyebrows, considered your third-eye chakra. As we've discussed, your third eye is considered the seat of your intuition, but it's also related to the pituitary gland. Your pituitary gland is considered the master gland and is responsible for the secretion of serotonin. Changes in serotonin levels in the brain can alter your mood, which is why the act of closing your eyes and letting your eyes look upward can have a tremendously relaxing effect.

If you have a few more minutes, then bring your hands together, fingers together and pointing upward, and press your thumbs on this third-eye point. Do nothing except press firmly (but not uncomfortably). Keep your eyes looking upward with your eyelids down. Breathe slowly and evenly for a few minutes.

Or, you can meditate on releasing expectations. Moms are always thinking about the future, often imagining that sometime in the future—*when all of their mothering challenges are successfully addressed*—happiness will come. This way of being focused on the future was likely learned by observing our mothers' thought processes, and it often becomes an unconscious habit.

To counteract this tendency, pause for a few minutes and sit quietly, or even lie down if possible. Breathe in and breathe out a few times, focusing solely on your breath. Quiet all mind chatter, and then bring your mind to the present, and use it to make a conscious decision to surrender the habit of focusing on the future. Choose to focus, instead, on what's happening right now and living more fully in the present. With your eyes closed, breathe in joy and peace . . . and then breathe out worry about the future. As you breathe, recognize that everything you need is already here, right now! Breathe in peace and joy . . . breathe out worrying about the future. The more you practice this meditation, the more you'll learn to focus on and live in the now, which is the foundation of real happiness.

Me-Time: Pamper Yourself

Having to wait an hour provides an opportunity to squeeze in a little me-time. Why not find a local spa or beauty shop and zip on over for a manicure or pedicure? Or, if the weather's amenable, take a stroll through the neighborhood, noticing landscapes you love or whatever draws your eye. If a friend lives nearby, you could plan ahead to stop by for tea. You could also listen to a book or music CD, whether through your car radio or your iPod, selecting something that no one likes but you, savoring your alone time.

When There's More Time

If you're going to spend a few hours waiting for practice to end or watching games, you can do any of the above or come up with even more ideas. If it's nice weather, take a stroll around the perimeters of the field or rink.

If you're feeling stressed or enduring mind chatter about all the things yet to be done that day, here's a calming meditation you could do on site:

Reclining pose is a great option when you have time to spare and your car available. Slide your seat back as far as it will go and recline. Bring your knees toward your chest, and place your feet on the dashboard (on either side of the steering wheel), or bring them up towards you chest, wrapping your arms around them. If you have one available, place a rolled towel or sweater behind your neck. If this doesn't work very well in your driver's seat, or if the posture leaves you feeling too exposed or vulnerable, move to the passenger side or the back seat.

Once you are comfortable, notice your energy and your inner dialogue. If your inner dialogue feels judgmental (of yourself or others), visualize your breath entering the dialogue. Search for words that bring peace to you. They could be: *It is not the end of the world if I do not watch this soccer practice,* or *I am not responsible for everyone's happiness.* Think or say these words several times to see if they help shift your inner dialogue, and remember that even a tiny shift will bring you peace.

LAST-RESORT MEDITATION

"No matter how old a mother is, she watches her middle-aged children for signs of improvement."

—FLORIDA SCOTT-MAXWELL

So you're finally home again, with minutes to spare before you have to start making dinner. If you're feeling frazzled, everyone might be happier if you took a few minutes to slip into your bedroom for a last-resort meditation.

Cleanse Your Energy

Take an energy cleansing "shower." Stand and imagine you have removed your clothing. Inhale and reach your arms up. Exhale and lower your arms to your sides, imagining a shower of sparkling gold light trickling over your body. Repeat the motion several times, allowing this gold light to cascade over your body and clean all of the negative energy you may be feeling or may have picked up during the day. Visualize the negative energy flowing away from you and being absorbed by the earth.

CHAPTER SUMMARY

Those few hours after school are often filled with a crush of activities that interfere with homework, making it difficult for moms to keep their children on track. Remember, there's no such thing as a perfect mom (or perfect children), and the best you can do is probably pretty spectacular. Here are a few suggestions we offered to help you successfully navigate these hours:

- Surrender any ideas of perfection!
- Encourage your kids to join you in tree pose to help everyone rebalance and regroup.
- Be a mindful mom, and take a few minutes to focus on each child.
- Younger children will take to yoga or tai chi like ducks to water, which opens the way to productive physical activity and occasions to discuss spiritual beliefs, whatever yours may be.
- Creating a mini-flow yoga opportunity that involves animal poses is really fun for kids.

- Stealing time, even if it's ten minutes, offers opportunities for you to gather your energy and focus on what needs to be done—as well as what could be enjoyed.
- Breathing exercises can help everyone remain calm and focused while addressing homework.
- You can make the most of extracurricular-activity runs if you take whatever time is available to squeeze in short meditations.

It's time for dinner and all the challenges that come with making, eating, and cleaning up afterward. There are, of course, many techniques for making the most of dinner, and we're ready to offer up all the servings you'll need.

4

Dinner

*"A good cook is like a sorceress
who dispenses happiness."*

—ELSA SCHIAPARELLI

Everyone's stomach is beginning to rumble, and you're in charge of dinner. Unless you're one of those moms who creates a monthly meal plan (does anyone do that, or is it some kind of urban myth?), you're likely scrambling for ideas—and time.

First things first, calm yourself, and then. . . .

CLAIM YOUR SPACE

"The fact is that it takes more than ingredients and technique to cook a good meal. A good cook puts something of himself into the preparation—he cooks with enjoyment, anticipation, spontaneity, and he is willing to experiment."

—PEARL BAILEY

Claiming your kitchen and the work you perform in it will help you remember the joy you take in feeding your family well. Yes, cooking can become drudgery, but it could also be viewed as your sacred contribution to your family's well-being. They may take you for granted, but you know deep within that it is a privilege and an honor to be given the responsibility of raising children—and children rely most on their mothers for proper nutrition. What you do sets the standard for the rest of their lives, and that is something to be taken very seriously.

Giving Thanks Meditation

A great way to claim your kitchen is to pause for a ritual, such as offering prayerful thanks. Before you start anything, light a candle, recognizing that you can *choose* to focus upon and experience thankful energy flowing throughout your body, appreciation for your place in the universe, and a joyful feeling for your current life situations.

Sit quietly, and breathe in and out slowly, until you quiet your mind and feel relaxed. Visualize, in as much detail as you are able, people whom you are grateful to have in your life. (If time permits, journaling can deepen this meditation.) Begin with those you love, and then extend your gratitude to anyone who has crossed your path in life and positively impacted you.

Visualize things that you are grateful to have in your life: your senses, blue sky, cool breezes, red wine, lobster, family, laughter, starry nights, full moons, vivid colors, music, washing machines, vacuums, fireplaces, and whatever comes to mind.

Visualize qualities you have that you are grateful are part of your total being: persistence, dedication, cheerfulness, intelligence, and so on. Bring your hands to a prayerful pose against your heart, and offer thanks for your many blessings.

Once you begin an exercise in gratitude, you begin to vibrate gratitude. Done often, it can become an extremely rewarding habit.

Me-Time: Have a Cocktail!

If you enjoy a glass of red wine, go ahead and pour yourself a glass, as long as you take a minute to mindfully notice the experience by savoring the taste, enjoying the deliciousness, and appreciating the luxury (even if it's an inexpensive wine!). Wine spritzers that mix wine with soda water are also fun. If you're making Mexican food, why not have a margarita or a mojito? We're not suggesting getting sloshed, which is never a good idea for a mom. The idea is to enjoy the time you're spending in the kitchen and to make preparing dinner something that also brings you pleasure. If your husband is at home, invite him into the kitchen to share a toast.

CREATE A CALM KITCHEN

"I don't have a nanny or a housekeeper, and I only have a cleaner for one hour each week. I finish work and go home. I cook the dinner. I run into Tesco and do the housework in the evening."

—VICTORIA BECKHAM

Instead of feeling harried, create the atmosphere you want. If you want to lighten up and be cheerful as you go about your duties, do whatever makes you happy in your own kitchen. As you clean away any dirty dishes and ready the ingredients for cooking, play music that makes you feel like singing along (or at least inspires you). While you're putting things in order, focus on pleasant thoughts, or spend a few minutes remembering happy times you spent in your mother's kitchen growing up.

Visualize Happy Memories

As you begin your work in the kitchen, spend a few minutes remembering and reconnecting with happy memories. Doing so will help calm and center you and help you feel positive about what you're doing.

Think about a time that made you feel particularly good. It could be watching your grandmother make Thanksgiving dinner and helping to stir the gravy, or helping your mother or father husk corn for corn-on-the-cob, or even the time that you had a friend over and ended up laughing over the carton of eggs you dropped on the floor.

Hold that memory in your mind. Remember the feelings and sensations. What did it look like and smell like? Who was there with you? Take a moment to really enjoy the memory, and then release it with a smile on your face.

Then, make a commitment to create those kinds of memories for your children. If you feel happy and send out the happy vibes, your children may be lured into the kitchen to hang out as you cook. If they do join you, give them age-appropriate tasks to do so they learn how to cooperate and make a contribution to family events. Yes, dinner is an event, even when it's rushed. Years later, when your children are long gone, you'll look back fondly on these memories, so play your part in making them the kind of memories you'd want them to cherish.

A few ideas for making it fun:

- Make a game out of setting the table, or use rhymes to help them learn how to set the table.
- Share memories you have of being with your mother, particularly funny memories.
- Sing songs together.
- Make cookies together, and let them lick the spoons!

Try a Cooking Meditation

Here's a meditation that can be fun and productive.

Chopping Vegetables Meditation

You could plan this "gift" meal with a lot of vegetables, with a lot of chopping. Chopping vegetables can be really relaxing and can itself be a mindful meditation that you do with your children. Use it when you're preparing a lot of vegetables for a stir-fry or similar meal.

Stand side by side with all of the vegetables laid out on the counter in front of you. First show your (age-appropriate) child how to chop carefully, and then place your hand over his and help him practice until you feel confident that he is capable of chopping without harming himself. When he is ready, give him a sharp knife and observe carefully as he practices. (Usually kids have chopping accidents because the knife is dull and they begin sawing and then slip and cut themselves.)

Line up the vegetables to chop. Make sure that you do this slowly and use all of your senses (remembering to teach your children how to focus on their senses, as well). Look at the colors of the vegetables: the bright orange of the carrots, the green of broccoli, or the white onion. Feel the vegetables the texture, the softness of the silky threads of corn-on-the-cob, the rough skin of carrots, or the bumpy eyes of a potato. When was the last time you really appreciated a vegetable?

As you chop an onion, enjoy the smell *and* how it stings your eyes after a while. Notice the great variety of herbs, and sample their different smells. Taste a raw vegetable now and then as you are chopping, and really appreciate the texture and taste. Sprinkle a little sea salt onto vegetables as you chop and enjoy the salty raw vegetable. Listen to the sound of the chopping and how it sounds different with each vegetable. While you are cooking, listen to the sounds of simmering or sautéing, and smell the food, savoring the scent of garlic, for example.

Take a moment to really appreciate and give gratitude to everyone who worked so that the food is available to you. Offer gratitude to the farmers and workers who sometimes get very little wages to harvest the food, those who work in factories to produce and prepare packaged food, the store clerk who sells the food, and so on. This could be a nice conversation with your child as you work together to prepare dinner. This should not be a lecture—just thoughts your children can ponder. The more they see you offering appreciation and gratitude, the more they will learn to appreciate their many blessings as well as the unknown people who contribute to their blessings.

Me-Time: Cook's Night Off

Now and then an evening gets so frazzled that the thought of fixing dinner and eating it with your family overwhelms you. So go ahead and order pizza (you can make it reasonably healthy by asking for light cheese and adding vegetables), sit back, and wait for the delivery person. You can even let everyone take slices to their bedrooms or wherever they choose to eat. You don't have to serve perfect meals every night, and sometimes you need a night off.

GRATITUDE AT THE TABLE

"Any ordinary favor we do for someone or any compassionate reaching out may seem to be going nowhere at first, but may be planting a seed we can't see right now. Sometimes we need to just do the best we can and then trust in an unfolding we can't design or ordain."

—SHARON SALZBERG

No matter their age, children always liven up the dinner table. Impatient toddlers can create quite a noisy ruckus, but teenagers can bring their own calamity to the table, by being argumentative or sullen. Even if you think you've gotten used to the scattered energy around the table, on some level it gets to you. You long for them to appreciate the care you put into making the meal and to be sociable and pleasant throughout dinner. Still, kids are kids. So if you want a peaceful table, help your children focus on gratitude.

Say Grace

Even if you're not religious, saying grace at dinner is a marvelous way to express gratitude for all your many blessings and to teach your children to be thankful for the bounty before them. You could create a ritual, such as lighting a candle, ringing a small bell, holding hands, or simply bowing heads to unify and focus the family on giving thanks. Each family member could have a special night to take charge of the dinnertime ritual, such as ringing the bell before offering grace. Welcome your children's spontaneous "prayers" (you can call them "intentions" if you prefer), as they're likely to come up with jewels. Make it okay to laugh, as nothing relieves stress or further bonds your family like laughter.

Practice the ABCs of Gratitude

The times when everyone is actually sitting down together for dinner can be great times to learn about and teach gratitude. Studies have shown that those who have the most gratitude are the happiest.

As you are having dinner, start with the letter "A" and think of something you are grateful for that starts with the letter "A." For example, "I am grateful for apples." Taking turns around the table, go on to the letter "B," and see how far you all can go until dinner is done. Try to make this game silly as well. Laughing together can be a beautiful memory for the kids.

Appreciate Each Other

Going around the table, tell each person what you appreciate about him or her. As the mom, you can start this gratitude exercise. Start with one child and talk about all of the wonderful qualities the child has. Encourage the rest of the family to join you. This will teach children to be charitable about their family members, especially if there is some sibling rivalry. Everyone gets a turn. Don't worry if someone just says one or two words. It takes time to teach about gratitude for others in the family. Each child will feel so great being talked about in such a positive and loving way. They will eventually want others to feel the same way and will begin to share their feelings of gratitude for the rest of the family. You could extend this to your pets, telling them how you feel grateful for their unconditional love. Give them an extra rubdown and a treat as you share your gratitude with them.

Plan Some Gift Giving

Another way to share your gratitude is to pay it forward—to perform small acts of kindness toward other people. Dinner is a good time to talk about how you could do this. For example, decide that you will give a gift to someone every day for a week (or as long as you would like). It can be anything. You could buy someone's coffee ahead of you in the coffee line. Just tell the cashier "That woman's coffee is on me," and smile at the person and offer her a great day. It feels really good to give gifts.

You could pick some flowers from your garden and take them to a neighbor. You could offer someone your seat on the bus. Encourage your kids to do the same. As small children watch you with your gift giving, they will want to "help" people to smile as well. The gift-giving practice may last well into their lives.

For older children, how about talking to them about a neighbor who may be having some difficulty? Maybe you could prepare extra dinner together and share it with your neighbor. This would be a really meaningful gift: for your older child to take to a neighbor a meal he helped prepare or to invite the neighbor to dinner. The gift-giving experience can be a way to find a deeper meaning in your life. Think of gifts that do not cost any money: a smile to a stranger, holding a door, or helping someone put groceries in the car. For a few dollars you could give a gift for no reason at all—just that you are thinking of them.

POSTDINNER MEDITATIONS

"To nourish children and raise them against odds is in any time, any place, more valuable than to fix bolts in cars or design nuclear weapons."

—MARILYN FRENCH

To make postdinner cleanup less stressful, teach your older children how to do the dishes. Even younger children can help clear the table, wipe it down, and put food back in the refrigerator. Working together, you'll get it done in a snap and you'll be ensuring that they develop habits that will help them as adults.

Then, slip away for a meditation or yoga pose that will aid your digestion.

Three-Part Breath

This breath will improve digestion as it is a gentle massage to your abdominal organs. When you inhale deeply, your diaphragm pushes or massages your lower organs, stimulating your digestive tract.

Lie down on a yoga mat or a rug. Bring one hand to your abdominal area and one hand to the center of your ribs. This breathing is done with long, slow, deep breaths. Inhale first into your abdomen, and let it expand into your hand. While still inhaling, let your breath expand your ribcage and then expand into your upper chest. Exhale, and let your abdomen soften, your ribs come together, and your upper chest relax. Stay with this three-part breath for a few minutes.

Wind Relieving Pose

This posture will stimulate your abdominal organs and digestive tract. If you do this every day, it can help bring back and maintain digestive health. This posture also gently stretches your lower back and keeps your vertebrae aligned.

Lie on your back on a rug or yoga mat. Press your heels down, lengthening as you flex your feet, creating a nice stretch for your back and hamstrings. Inhale, bringing your breath down into your belly. As you exhale, bring your right knee up toward your chest. Wrap your fingers around the front of your knee. Continue breathing deeply. As you inhale, release your knee slightly, and as you exhale, draw your knee firmly toward your chest, keeping your extended left foot flexed (toes pulled toward your forehead). Repeat a few times with your breath.

This movement will massage the ascending colon. (Always start with the right knee as this is the direction of movement in the colon.)

Reverse sides. Bring your left knee up toward your chest, and wrap your fingers around your left knee. Breathe deeply. As you inhale, slightly release the hold on your left knee, and as you exhale, draw the knee firmly in toward your chest. This will stimulate the descending colon. Keep your extended right foot flexed. This is very effective and should be done for several minutes.

When you are done with both sides, bring both your knees up toward your chest and wrap your arms around your knees. Give yourself a big hug, and gently roll from side to side.

Digestive Delight

A yoga pose known as the *spinal twist* also helps relieve constipation and improve digestion. It's a great pose to do before bed, particularly if you've eaten a heavy meal. (If you have a slipped or herniated disk, be very careful or avoid this posture.)

Sit down on a rug or yoga mat, and extend your legs. Bend your right knee, and cross the right foot over the left leg. Your right knee is pointed upward, and your right foot is on the mat near your left knee. Make sure that your spine is lengthened and you are not slumping. Press evenly through your sitting bones so that you feel your weight evenly distributed. If your spine rounds, sit on a folded blanket to tilt your hips forward and help lengthen and straighten your spine.

As you slowly inhale, wrap your left arm around your right knee. As you exhale, bring your right fingertips to the floor behind your hips, and look over your right shoulder. While maintaining the twist, breathe deeply in and out several times, and then repeat the same motions on the other side.

LAST-RESORT MEDITATION

"When my kids become wild and unruly, I use a nice,
safe playpen. When they're finished, I climb out."

—ERMA BOMBECK

When it comes to dinner, moms often need a break. All of your strategies work most days, but on this day, things are simply not going well. Moms should never feel guilty about any frustration or disappointment that arises when dinnertime becomes more of a headache than a pleasure. What's needed are last-resort alternatives, such as time-outs—for you and for your kids. If your children need a time-out, have them go into another room until they calm down and can behave properly. If they are upset and crying, sit with them and encourage them to breathe. Often children are simply overstimulated, or exhausted, which unfortunately comes out in unwelcomed behaviors. Offer them reassurance and comfort, and they'll likely recoup fairly quickly.

Time-Out for You

To give yourself a break and help you keep a leash on your frustration and stress, take this special time-out for yourself. Lean back against a wall, and press the back of your body toward the wall. Feel supported by the wall. Focus on your breath. Try to observe the flow of emotions. See if you can identify what emotion is present. Breathe into the emotion to see what is happening right now. Take a few more breaths. Consider: what is the best way to handle this for you and your child or family? What can you do to preserve the family unit (right now), to help the situation, and to accept responsibility as the parent?

When you come to a place of peace and insight, rejoin your children. Trust that you will know what to do to help them also come to a place of peace. As you come to a place of calm, your children will feel it (even if they only feel it on a subconscious level) and will begin to feel calm as well.

Staying Balanced with Moody Teenagers

Some of the most effective strategies for dealing with sulky or rebellious teenagers include ignoring their behavior (as long as it's possible, anyway), killing them with kindness, or making them laugh. The point is to not buy into their negative moods or reinforce their bad manners. It's a fine line for moms, but the main thing is to stay calm and mindful.

If you need a breather to calm down, remove yourself from the situation, and slow down your breathing until you feel calmer.

Go to your sacred space and meditate. Often all you need to do is release pent-up feelings, let go of any resentments over mishaps that occurred as you made or served dinner, and re-center yourself so you can enjoy the meal—and your family's company.

As you release your feelings of frustration, take a step back and remind yourself that the present may feel stressful but in the future you'll look back at these times with fondness. Reflect on your own teenage years, remembering how close to the surface your emotions felt in those years and how difficult it was for you to keep perspective. Repeat an affirmation or intention about engaging mindfully with your teenager. For example, you could say "My teen needs me to model calmness so that she can learn to regulate her own emotions," or "I will go forward from a place of stillness to engage thoughtfully with my child."

Phone Call Meditation

Think of your vocation of motherhood as sacred, challenging, and rewarding, and it will be that. You need the support of a cherished relationship. Find a friend whom you can trust, with whom you can speak candidly and truthfully, someone who is caring and has a genuine concern for your needs and feelings and has a sense of humor. How great to be able to laugh at yourself and not take yourself too seriously.

A true friend will encourage, accept, and support you, no matter what is happening in your life. We all have a need for true friendship, to receive it and to give it as well. Once you have a trusted friend, you can pre-arrange a convenient time for a phone conversation, or occasionally call her when emotional emergencies occur. Always make sure you are comfortable, maybe with your feet elevated and a cup of tea within reach before placing the call. Don't use the phone call as an opportunity to vent; think of it as a meditation, a talking meditation that will help you relieve stress and feel grounded. Choose to mindfully talk with your friend, asking for her support during a stressful time, mindfully connecting with someone who understands and cares about you.

CHAPTER SUMMARY

Whew, you not only survived the dinner hour—you enjoyed it! As the midnight hour approaches, let's review what you've learned in this chapter:

- Claiming your space and focusing on the nurturing aspects of providing dinner for your family will turn it from a chore to a pleasure.
- A happy cook creates happy meals, and we don't mean of the McDonald's variety. Make cooking something you enjoy doing, and everyone will enjoy and appreciate your efforts more.
- Invite your children to share the experience and to teach them useful life skills, such as cooking, setting the table, cleaning up after meals, and so on.
- Creating dinnertime rituals is a lovely way to strengthen the family bonds. Saying grace or having conversations about gratitude and giving are opportunities to deepen your children's empathy for others.
- If all the relaxation exercises in the world aren't doing the trick, give up and order pizza!
- After dinner, you can facilitate the digestive process with several yoga poses.

Hopefully, you'll have an hour or two before bedtime begins. If so, do something relatively relaxing, knowing that bedtime help is just one page away.

5

Bedtime

*"Problems always look smaller after a warm meal
and a good night's sleep."*

—ANONYMOUS

At last your day is truly winding down. Everyone has been fed, homework is done, and the kids are beginning to rub their eyes. You're optimistic that the regular bedtime ritual will go smoothly, and then . . . a fight breaks out between siblings, your oldest child realizes that he forgot to do his history assignment, and your toddler reaches critical mass,—all of which signals a rockier bedtime than normal.

Even if you're exhausted, getting the kids safely and smoothly off to bed has to be done. The good news is that a little private time lies on the horizon.

CREATE SOOTHING BEDTIME RITUALS

"A ruffled mind makes a restless pillow."

—CHARLOTTE BRONTË

Creating bedtime rituals for everyone is a great way to stay calm and centered and to help everyone get off to sleep without stress. If you institute a ritual when your children are young, it will serve you well as they get older, too. But you can start bedtime rituals at any age; you just have to be consistent. Creating rituals also helps you and your children stay mindful and in the present moment. Giving your child a bath, reading a story, and tucking her in bed are all actions that can build your connection with your child and can be meditations in themselves.

Mindful Mom

If your children are under the age of five, bath time offers a precious mindful-mom moment. Children rarely need scrubbing to get clean, and a gentle washing with a soft washcloth can feel absolutely marvelous, particularly to their young skin. As you help them bathe, gently brush their skin with the washcloth or with your hands, thinking back to when you first brought them home and how often you cuddled or caressed them. If you slow down bath time a smidge, you can evoke those first bonding moments for both of you. There's nothing quite as soothing, healing, or loving as a mother's gentle touch. Enjoy!

Bedtime Meditations for Kids

Bedtime is an ideal time for meditation. Begin with something really simple, such as focusing on breath. Ask your child if he can hear his breath. Tell him to breathe noisily. Ask him to do this a few times. Now ask him to breathe really quietly, and show him how to breathe into his belly and to blow out all the air. Have him breathe again and again. Tell him that breathing this way and focusing on his breath will naturally clear his mind and help him feel calm.

When your child is relaxed, ask her what she would like to have happen the next day. Help her choose one activity or event that she's eager to experience. Then, help her learn how to visualize the event as if it is already happening. Have her describe where it would take place, who would be there, how each person would behave, and how she would feel when everything went exactly as planned—or better. When she has completed her visualization, tell her it's now time to close her eyes and drift off to dreamland, where she can revisit her visualization.

Tense and Release

If your child is still wired, you can teach him how to tense and release. Lie next to your child so that you can model how to tense and release all your muscles. Begin by asking your child to pay attention to his breathing. Is it fast, or slow? Close your eyes, and breathe slowly in and out, drawing your breath into your tummy and then slowly blowing out all of the air. Then, say (and model) these guiding steps:

1. Start with your toes. Tense or curl your toes under, inhale, and then relax your toes as you exhale.

2. Tense your feet by pretending you are pointing your toes toward your forehead and pushing your heels away. Inhale while they are tense, and as you exhale, relax your feet.

3. Tense or squeeze your buttocks (kids love this word and will likely giggle when you say it) and your entire legs, feet, and toes at the same time. Inhale, and as you exhale, release your buttocks (another giggle), legs, feet, and toes.

4. Pull your stomach in tight, until your ribcage is sticking out; bring your shoulders up to your ears. Inhale, and as you exhale, relax your tummy and your shoulders.

5. Clench your arms and your hands (making a tight fist), lifting them about 1 or 2 inches off the bed. Inhale, and as you exhale, relax your arms and hands, gently dropping them back on the bed.

6. Close your eyes really tight, and close your mouth really tight. Inhale, and as you exhale, relax your face.

7. Clench your entire body including your buttocks (giggle) and face and inhale. Hold this for a few seconds, and then, as you exhale, say a really long "Ahhhhhhhh."

By now, your child should feel more relaxed, but if not, try some yoga meditations.

Calming Bedtime Yoga Meditations to Do with Your Kids

Bedtime is a perfect time to introduce yoga meditation into your children's lives. If you start when they're still little, they'll readily embrace it. You can explain concepts to fit their age and interest, describing the mechanics of the pose and its benefits (that it helps your tummy relax, for example), or you can make it a silly game, seeing if they can wriggle themselves into and out of yoga poses.

Rag Doll Pose

Rag doll is a fun—and mindful!—pose that would be great for your child to do before he actually gets into the bed. You can do the pose with your child to show him.

Stand up really straight, with your knees slightly bent or just soft. Bring your arms upward as you inhale, and as you exhale, gently fold over just like a rag doll, allowing your arms, hands, and fingers to loosely hang. It is not important to try to touch your toes. Rag doll is about just hanging. If your child needs better instruction, first tell her to pretend she is a pair of pants folded over a hanger, and then a rag doll hanging over a railing. Ask her to visualize what the rag doll would look like. Then ask her to imagine how a rag doll would breathe, what it would sound like. Then have both of you inhale through your noses, and then say "Ahhhhhh" as you exhale through your mouths. Stay for a few breaths, inhaling through your nose and exhaling by saying "Ahhhh" through your mouth. To make it even more mindful, tell your child that you are doing the pose to learn how to let everything else go and focus on only one thing, which in this case is total relaxation.

Child's Pose

Another great pose to make part of a bedtime ritual is child's pose. Begin by having your child come to hands and knees on the bed.

1. Have your child inhale, and when she exhales, help her lower her hips down to rest on her heels.
2. Have her stretch her arms straight down by her sides, palm sides up, and tell her to keep her forehead gently resting on the bed.
3. Ask your child to make herself really small and watch her curl up even more.

Once she's in child's pose, you can place your hand on her back and gently roll her from side to side, about 2 inches and no more. You want it to be a soothing rock from side to side. She will love the warmth and healing touch of your hand on her back. Touch her with the intention to offer calming and soothing energy, and ask her to focus on the sensations.

Cobbler's Pose

Another relaxing pose to try is cobbler's pose. Have your child lie down in bed on his back, bend his knees bringing his feet closer to his hips, and then open his knees to each side. To make it more comfortable, you can put a pillow under each knee. This pose helps your child calm himself. While he's in the pose, either read to him or have him read a book on his own.

Saying Goodnight

It's also helpful to create a ritual for saying goodnight. Whether they'll admit it or not, children love being literally tucked in. If you garnish it with a kiss, a gentle touch, a ruffling of his hair, and something you always say, your child will grow to love and take comfort in this moment. While we don't recommend "Don't let the bedbugs bite," we find "I love you more than the sun, the moon, and the stars" to be about right. Whatever you choose, make it special and filled with love.

Me-Time: Slip Into Your Favorite Pajamas

Moms need time to prepare for bed, too, so why not slip away for a few minutes to slip into your favorite pajamas, whether they're wispy cotton or snuggly flannel? As you change, take a moment to smooth a refreshing, scented (or unscented) oil or lotion over your arms, legs, neck, and back. Pause to take a breath and inhabit your body fully. Notice any tension, and use your touch to gently massage painful areas. End by massaging your feet and then your hands with lotion or oil. Using your thumb to massage your hands is very relaxing. If you have a partner, give each other a mini-massage; since the kids are already tucked in bed, anything goes!

HOW TO HANDLE OFF NIGHTS

"Come, cuddle your head on my shoulder, dear,
Your head like the golden-rod,
And we will go sailing away from here
To the beautiful land of Nod."

—ELLA WHEELER WILCOX

All children occasionally have a bad night, times when they have trouble falling asleep. Rather than letting the situation get out of hand, spend a few minutes with your child to find out if worries are keeping her awake. Maybe she needs a little extra "mom time" to clear her mind. First, ask if she's worried about anything, and listen closely to what she says. Even if she's not sure, she'll likely give you clues about what's really bothering her. After you talk, suggest a meditation to help her quiet her mind.

Using Memories as Meditation

If your child is having trouble sleeping, it often helps to focus on past memories, particularly ones that tap into times when he felt safe, happy, and loved. Here's how:

- Crawl in bed or sit beside your child and whisper or speak softly, asking him to remember a time when he was particularly happy. If it was during your last vacation by the sea, ask softly "Do you remember the cottage we rented on the shore?"

- Pause for a few breaths, giving him time to remember. Let him talk about it if he chooses, encouraging him to talk softly and slowly. If memories don't spring to mind for him, gently ask what was his favorite part of the cottage (the bunk beds or the screened-in porch?).

- Ask him to close his eyes as he thinks back to those happy days, and then gently ask if he can see the cottage in his imagination, see the little room where he slept, hear the sound of the waves coming to shore, remember the taste of the salty sea. Pause for a few breaths to let him form pictures in his mind.

- To draw him deeper into the meditation, ask if he remembers the weather: "Was it hot? Was it cloudy? Did it rain all week? Do you remember how it smelled after the rain? Do you remember how the clouds were bigger than we'd ever seen? How we saw angels and sea horses and sailing ships in the clouds?"

- Encourage more happy memories by asking if he remembers how the sand felt on his feet and how it squished between his toes. Does he remember how much fun it was to ride the waves? How the ocean was cold and the sand was warm?

- Continue talking or whispering, softly and slowly. When your child whispers in reply, you can slow your breathing down and whisper "Hhhoooommme" ("home") as you exhale, replicating the sound of the ocean waves as they come to shore. When your child notices your soft breath, consciously or unconsciously, he may begin to breathe the same way. If he doesn't, you can encourage him to listen and join in with you as you mimic the waves.

- Keep breathing slowly in and out, saying "Hhhooommme" (this is called *ujjayi* or *ocean breath*) as you exhale. Soon your child will feel so relaxed that he will drift blissfully off to sleep—like a bottle on a gently rolling sea.

Ujjayi (Ocean) Breath

Ujjayi breath is a very calming breath that sounds like the ocean or the sound you would hear if you put your ear next to a seashell. To achieve this breath, softly draw out the word "home" as you exhale ("Hhhhoooommme"). Say this word in a whisper. Now say it as you round and gently close your mouth. You can also reverse and draw in the word. It may sound like Darth Vader, only much softer and less scary.

TIME FOR YOU TO GO TO BED!

"To achieve the impossible dream, try going to sleep."

—JOAN KLEMPNER

At last, the kids are all asleep, and you are looking forward to bed . . . but all of a sudden, just when your time becomes your own to relax, thoughts start whizzing through your head at the speed of light. You've fallen prey to worrying about what comes tomorrow, or fretting over what you could have done better today. What you need is extended me-time, beginning with a relaxing bath.

Take a Nice, Long Bath

There's nothing lovelier or more refreshing and relaxing than a hot bath. The warmth of the water helps your muscles release the day's tension, and the luxury leaves you feeling deliciously sensual, particularly if you use scented bath oils and create an ambience. As always, candles or low lighting and soft music will set the right tone. Then, try a sensual bath meditation to keep your focus where it belongs: on your beautiful body.

Sensual Meditation for the Bath

Turn off overhead lights and light a few candles. Add a fragrant bath oil or bath salts, and play soft, soothing music, if you like.

1. Once you are in the water, take a few deep breaths and exhale with a soothing "Ahhhhhhh." Notice how light your body feels when submerged in the water.

2. Imagine the water washing away the stresses of the moment so you can emerge feeling refreshed and rested.

3. Say a prayer of gratitude for the bath and for the clean water. A prayer of gratitude can be as simple as "Thank you for the bath."

4. Use all of your senses while in the tub. Notice how the water ripples when you move your arms or legs. Focus on the ripples and the bouncing reflections of light they create.

5. Lie still until the water stills. Allow the warm water to hug your body, noticing how comfortable your body feels clothed in water.

6. Spend the next few minutes offering prayers of gratitude for the beauty of your body, for the way in which your body serves you. Begin the prayer of gratitude with your feet.

7. Think about how your feet take you on the journey through your life, how they are able to support the rest of your body. Look down at those amazing feet, and invite your foot muscles to relax.

8. Next, consider your legs. Notice your calves, lifting one leg at a time just to watch the water run off. Notice the beautiful curve of your calves, and give thanks to your legs for the work they do for you. If you notice any critical thoughts entering, politely invite them to leave. Imagine the warm water caressing your legs, improving circulation. Take a few deep breaths, and end by saying "Ahhhhhhh."

9. Notice your hips and belly, and offer them an extra prayer of gratitude. If your amazing body has given birth to your children, offer a prayer of gratitude to your hips and belly. Marvel at the miracle of childbirth, and honor your body's contribution. If you haven't given birth, your lap has held your children close; pause to feel those marvelous gifts. Draw in another deep breath, ending with "Ahhhh."

10. Notice the beautiful colors of your body, the warm skin tones, the rosy blush forming from the warmth of the water. Honor your body as a work of art.

11. Lift your arms out of the water, and look at them, noticing how the steam rises off them. Stroke your arms gently with your hands, thanking them for their strength.

12. Bring your focus to your hands, offering them a special prayer of gratitude. Your hands contain and transmit so much loving energy, and their touch offers love and healing to your family. They hold, hug, and comfort your children and others whom you love. They cook and clean and do a myriad of things that help you care for those you love.

13. Gently stroke your face with your hands. This is the face your husband and children love. Offer thanks to your face, your smile, your eyes.

14. Bring your palms together, and lower them to your chest, pressing your thumbs into your heart center in a final prayer of gratitude.

15. Before you end your bath, close your eyes, and smell the scent of the soap or oil you are using. Listen to the water as you slowly move around. After the water begins to cool, prepare to slowly surrender your bath.

16. When you are ready, wrap yourself in a thirsty towel, and slather lotion on your arms and legs and everywhere you want to retain moisture.

17. Before you slip into your nightgown or pajamas, lift your arms up and over your head, gently arching your back while you enjoy a few more "Ahhhhh" breaths. Enjoy the rest of the night feeling relaxed, scented, and rejuvenated.

CREATE YOUR OWN BEDTIME RITUAL

"When I was a kid, I'd kneel down at the side of my bed every night before I went to sleep, and my mother and I would say a Greek prayer to the Virgin Mary."

—OLYMPIA DUKAKIS

Just as rituals help your children settle in for sleep, having a bedtime routine (sacred or otherwise) can also help you. A bedtime ritual can be whatever helps you relax and turn off your overactive mind at night: perhaps reading a novel for half an hour, or listening to soothing music, or drinking a cup of chamomile tea. Of course there's always a romp in the proverbial hay with your lover, at least when you're in the mood.

In-Out Meditation

This meditation is simple and traditional.

1. Begin by sitting in a comfortable seated posture on your floor, rug, or yoga mat.
2. Lift your hips up a tiny bit so that your knees are in alignment with your hips. If needed, place a small pillow or a rolled towel under your hips.
3. Lengthen your spine and bring your chin toward your chest so that the crown of your head is reaching upward.
4. As you slowly breathe in, say "In."
5. As you slowly breathe out, say "Out."

That's it. Seems simple, and it is. Simple does not mean easy. As your mind wanders, gently but firmly bring it back to focusing solely on the In-Out breath. Replace your thoughts with your breath. Stay for five minutes to start, and work your way up to ten minutes. Learning to quiet your mind and focus on your breath is key to mindfulness, and you may enjoy this place of "nonthinking" so much that you will want to remain in this meditation for longer periods of time.

When you are ready to come out of the meditation, open your eyes, breathe normally for a few breaths, and go to bed.

Object Meditation

This meditation can help you quiet your mind and bring your focus back to you. Find an object that is beautiful or interesting to you. It can be a shell or a religious icon or a piece of your mother's jewelry or a perfume bottle she gave you that you always loved—anything that is meaningful to you.

1. Place the object in front of you, positioned so that you are able to be seated with your eyes gazing forward at the object.
2. Keep your eyes focused on the object without looking away.
3. Begin to breathe deeply, transitioning into long, slow breaths that you draw deeply into your belly, slowly and fully.
4. Keep your every thought on the physical aspects of the object—the texture, size, color . . . all awareness rests on the physical aspects of the object. When your mind wanders, notice what it wanders to, and then bring it back to the object.
5. Once you feel calm and focused, close your eyes and try to "see" the object in your mind's eye. If you lose your concentration, open your eyes, study the object, and then try again.

Stay with this meditation for five minutes, or as long as you'd like.

LAST-RESORT MEDITATION

"A further sign of health is that we don't become undone by fear and trembling, but we take it as a message that it's time to stop struggling and look directly at what's threatening us."

—PEMA CHÖDRÖN

If it's been a rough day, full of little mishaps and problems galore, and it's well past your bedtime and none of your usual calming rituals have worked, you need a last-resort meditation. Sometimes writing about your horrible, no-good, very bad day can help you shed the tension; and sometimes there's little to do but pray that tomorrow is much, much brighter. You can also try a simple yoga meditation designed to relax body and mind.

Legs Up the Headboard

Hop into bed and swing your legs up, resting them gently against the headboard (or wall). Squiggle closer until your bottom is as close as is comfortably possible to the headboard. Have your arms by your sides, palms facing up.

Lift your hips by bending your knees and pressing your feet onto the headboard. When you lift your hips, slide a pillow under your lower back and the top of your hips to lift them up, so your tailbone curls over the pillow. You want to have a gentle lift of your hips that also allows your lower back to tilt toward the mattress. Your back should feel as if it is arched naturally, and not a strong arch. Then straighten your legs, and stay in this position, allowing the blood to rush out of your feet, legs, and hips, giving your heart a rest. This pose will relieve tired legs and mild backaches, as well as provide a gentle stretch for the backs of your legs. It's also the perfect time to breathe in and out, focusing your mind on the renewing energy that comes with breath, and then focusing on the calm and relaxation that come with quieting the mind and focusing on your breath. Breathe in peace; breathe out frustration.

Stay in this position for ten to fifteen minutes while you practice long, slow breaths. This is also a nice pose to practice gratitude by saying a prayer of thanksgiving. If you can truly feel thankful for a bad day, you will be on your way to enjoying a really good sleep.

CHAPTER SUMMARY

In this chapter, you learned how to create an environment where everyone is encouraged to calmly go to sleep in order to be well rested and to tackle the next day with enthusiasm. Here are some of the strategies we discussed:

- Adhering to a bedtime routine makes it easier for everyone.
- The tense-and-release exercise will help everyone release muscle tension.
- Rag doll pose is a great way to shake out resistance and help your kids relax.
- Soothing meditations, such as guided memory meditations, can help kids transition from hyperactivity to restful sleep.
- A delicious, soothing, hot bath meditation can improve your sleep—and boost your sensuality!
- It's also important that moms have their own bedtime rituals, activities that help you transition from your busy day to a quieted mind and body.

Next we'll enter Part 2, where we'll discuss situations that don't occur every day, such as hobbies, activities, weekends, and those oh-so-lovely vacations.

PART 2

MEDITATIONS FOR SPECIAL OCCASIONS

This part of the book will focus on things that don't necessarily happen every day but that happen often enough to create challenges for busy moms. These activities range from extracurricular activities and sports to hobbies, as well as those on weekends and vacations. Even though many of these activities are great fun, they also contribute to the busyness and exhaustion that moms endure.

Throughout the next three chapters, we'll offer many more ideas for you, as well as methods to steal a little "me-time" whenever possible.

We'll also provide meditations and yoga poses that will lift you up and keep you ready to enjoy your life, whenever you have the opportunity. Many of the meditations and exercises will build on what you've already learned, offering new spins or deepening your experience.

By the end of the book, you will have a whole new lease on motherhood . . . we promise!

6

Weekends

"You must learn how to validate and give yourself permission to feel; in order to do this, you must create the space for that emotion in your life."

—SIERRA BENDER

Finally, the weekend rolls around, and you get a break in the action . . . or do you? If you're a working mom, you may at least have a few days off from the daily grind, but all moms end up working all weekend. As much as you'd love to have the luxury of time to simply be and relax, moms rarely get time off from being, well, mom.

If you're like most moms, you likely spend a portion of your weekends tackling laundry, running errands, getting the house in order, paying bills, catching up with family, and handling all the normal activities that occur in households where children reside. And there are always activities, from playdates to sporting events.

Even if you're not working outside your home, weekends present their own challenges. At the forefront of those challenges is the long list of errands that must be run; so just as you have to do, let's start there and quickly move on to more fun activities, ones that will involve more me-time for you!

CONSULT YOUR HIGHER SELF BEFORE RUSHING ABOUT

"Stress is basically a disconnection from the earth, a forgetting of the breath. Nothing is that important. Just lie down."

—NATALIE GOLDBERG

Before you go rushing about, take time to meditate on needs versus desires. Instead of succumbing to busyness, meditate on identifying essentials, what truly must be done, and releasing chores that can wait or can be discarded altogether.

Meditations for Learning to Slow Down

How many lists do we make in our lives? We get ambitious and create a picture of how we want things to look, instead of seeing how they actually are. If we learn to slow down our lives, things will become more relaxed and clear. When we are busy, we are focused on the future: what things could be, what we could have, or what we could or should do. We lose sight of the here and now.

Learning to go about daily chores mindfully can help you learn to slow down. Choose normal, everyday things that you would normally do, but do them really slowly. This changes your focal point from "What is the next task or thing or sensation?" to the moment of concentration. It takes concentration to move slowly, mindfully, and the focus brings your attention to what is happening in the moment. To slow down is to honor each and every moment we have. We cannot count on our next breath, really. We only have the breath that we are breathing.

As you are slowing down, you may begin to realize that your mind is always consumed by thoughts of the past or the future and is rarely in the moment. Doing things slowly brings your focus to the moment, making whatever you do a meditation. Slow moving creates (with practice) a calmer mind. Slow moving helps you notice the tiny details that you usually miss.

Eat Slowly

Eat your next meal very slowly. Make a place at your table, and sit down to eat. Look at your food, pausing to breathe, noticing the smell, the textures, the colors. Even if it is a very simple and ordinary meal, you can savor the beauty and delight of it. Even a plain bowl of oatmeal is a thing of beauty when you slow down and really look at it. Consider how it was created. How amazing is it that food emerges from the ground? Food actually growing! Bow your head in gratitude for the food, pick up your fork, and take a bite. Let the food linger on your tongue for a few seconds before you begin to chew. Chew slowly, for a long time, and really taste each bite. You may think something is bland, and with further investigation you realize that it's actually sweet. Eat your entire meal like this, slowly and mindfully.

Pray Slowly

Come to a comfortable cross-legged posture on a rug or a yoga mat. Inhale and exhale slowly, until it feels very natural. Shake your hands rapidly, and then rest your hands on your knees, palms upward. Bring all of your awareness to your fingertips. Feel the tip of each and every finger and thumb. As you think of each finger, move it just slightly. You may feel almost a pulse at your fingertips or a throbbing sensation. Very slowly lift your hands off your knees, bringing them toward each other very slowly. Feel as though the space between your hands is thick. Move as slowly as you are able, as though your hands were moving themselves. Notice the tiniest detail of the movement. Bring your hands together in front of your heart center, and press your thumbs into the center of your sternum. Stay for a few minutes in slowness. When you are ready, pray slowly, with true intention.

Slowing down can bring you to a place of acceptance—acceptance of who you are and what you have, acceptance of your family, your friends, your financial situation, your community, and the world. Slowing down can become a meaningful, mindful practice.

Me-Time: Swap Time with Friends

All moms have a multitude of errands to run, so why not team up with your friends to share errands? A friend could pick up your dry cleaning (and hers) while you pick up her kids (and yours) from soccer. Or do a child-care swap: on Saturday you watch your friend's kids for two hours, and on Sunday she watches your kids for two hours. Or swap dinner: you cook enough dinner for both families on Saturday, and she returns the favor on Sunday. That way you can both steal time for a pedicure, or to have coffee with another friend—or with your husband. Also, consider hiring a handyman or a local teen to help with household chores, like raking leaves or mowing the lawn.

Reward Yourself

One of the best motivations to get the undesirable errands done is to dream up a reward. Let's say you dread grocery shopping (because the grocery store is always ridiculously crowded on weekends) and taking the dogs to the groomer (because the dogs hate going to the groomer and always behave badly). Tell yourself that the minute you've accomplished those goals, you'll drop by the local farmers' market to pick up fresh green beans, a few ripe peaches, and a croissant. Or better yet, you'll find two hours for a massage or a spa treatment. Whatever reward you choose, make sure it involves pleasure for *you*.

Another reward, of course, is to take twenty minutes to meditate. Ideally you would use this time to focus on your inner feelings and desires, what's occurring in your life that brings you great pleasure or that causes you pain. Think of it as a tune-up that will keep your mom engine purring right along, without sacrificing your needs, your wants, your hopes and dreams. An intuition meditation could set the stage nicely, as weekends are the perfect time to meditate on what you want to happen in the coming week (and months) for you—and you alone!

Meditations for Tapping Into Your Intuition

As we mentioned earlier, your intuition is related to the area of your third eye, which is located between your eyebrows. This area is considered a chakra (a swirling circle of energy) that is connected to your pineal gland, located behind and above your pituitary gland, near the center of your brain. The pineal gland has characteristics like an eye: it has a lens and is sensitive to light. According to many ancient traditions, your third eye has special powers and is linked to a higher consciousness. You are able to stimulate this center of intuition a few ways:

- Bring your hands together, and press your thumbs firmly into the space between your eyebrows. Close your eyes, and look up into that same space. Inhale and exhale deeply. Stay for a few minutes. After about three minutes, bring your hands down and keep your eyes closed. Thoughts, sensations, and even images may appear. Just notice what your third eye reveals. If you don't feel anything, be patient. Intuition takes time to develop.

- Slowly speaking the sound of "Om" (a universal sound that is also used to start and close yoga practice, discussed in Chapter 1) will stimulate your third-eye chakra. Inhale deeply, and as you exhale, round your mouth slowly, allowing the sound to vibrate in your chest, as you draw it out, saying "OOOOOOOOOMMMMMMMMM." The vibration will stimulate your third eye and open your center of intuition.
- Come on to your belly with your arms by your sides and your legs extended. Press your forehead (third-eye point) on the mat, and just stay in this position for a while; or come to child's pose (on your hands and knees, resting your hips down on your heels, as described in Chapter 5), and press your forehead on the mat. If this bothers your neck, stack your hands, palm sides up, and rest your third eye on your palm.

Opening to the possibilities of intuition can bring you to a deeper connection to your spiritual body. If you do not practice a religion, consider opening to the possibility. If you do practice an organized religion, this third-eye opening can bring you to a deeper prayer life.

Say a Little Prayer

Prayers can be considered wishes or intentions. If you're not used to saying prayers, start by saying prayers that you may already know, such as the Lord's Prayer or Hail Mary. Say the words slowly, really listening to the sound and the meaning of the words. If you feel connected to a prayer, repeat the same prayer a few times, or even for fifteen minutes or so. If the prayer doesn't resonate with you, make up your own prayer (or prayerful intention). Write down the prayer or intention, and say it often throughout the day. This could become a family practice. You could introduce the practice by having your children say bedtime prayers as a family ritual. You can also pray before meals, or before everyone leaves the house each morning. Sharing prayerful intentions is a lovely way to offer blessings to family, even if it's as simple as saying "God bless Mom, Dad, Grandma, sister, teacher," and so on.

GO OUT TO DINNER—WITH GROWNUPS!

*"Who among us has the extra time
to not live every moment fully?"*

—JUDITH HANSON LASATER

You don't have to spend every night eating with the kids. After all, moms (and dads) deserve an adult night out. In fact, if you're married or in a long-term partnership, you need the time to nurture your relationship. You may want to go with a friend to nurture that relationship. If you're single, take time to go on a date!

Whether it's a spur-of-the-moment decision (thankfully the babysitter is available on short notice), or a planned event, dining out is always fun. Take time to primp. How about having the sitter come early so you can take a mindful shower?

Start with a Mindful Shower Meditation

As discussed in Chapter 1, taking a luxurious shower is a fabulously refreshing thing to do before you start your day or go on a date. Taking a mindful shower, focused on how the pelting water can wash away any minor frustrations and awaken your nerve endings for the evening ahead is an even richer meditation. Spending a bit more time and focusing on your sensuality will make this shower the perfect precursor to a romantic evening.

To take a mindful shower, you want to first clear your mind of any distractions, and then to move slowly, enjoying each sensation as it occurs. If it helps, state your intention clearly: "I am shedding all of my worries to focus on my sensuality."

1. Begin by stepping into the shower. How does it feel going from dry to totally wet? Are the physical sensations pleasant or unpleasant? Stand still for a few minutes, letting the water run over you, quieting all thoughts, experiencing the rejuvenating powers of warm water.

2. Turn your attention to your feelings. How does it feel to have peace and quiet? Breathe in relaxation, and breathe out frustration. Notice as worries dissipate and how it feels when muscle tension subsides. Notice how unadulterated bliss feels in your body.

3. Notice all sensations, such as the lavender fragrance in your soap, the citrus in your shampoo, the grainy texture of your face scrub. Allow the smells and textures to conjure up pleasant memories. Listen to the water as it cascades over your head and hair. What does it sound like? Listen as the water

drops strike the shower curtain or the glass. How does it sound different from when it hits the shower tiles? As steam fills the shower stall, does it make you want to draw swirls on the walls as a small child would? Give it a try!

4. Dismiss all other thoughts. If thoughts about what comes after your shower or what happened earlier come up, gently brush them aside, and stay focused on sensations occurring in the shower. Stay fully present, living breath to breath, sensation to sensation.

5. As your shower nears its end, try humming. It not only feels good, it can sound comforting to you, and to your family if they hear you. Feel the vibrations in your throat as you hum, and attune yourself to this feeling. Often you can recall those sensations later to supersede unkind words you may use throughout the day particularly if you learn to associate kind words with the feeling of humming. Practice by saying kind words for yourself, such as: "May the words I use to describe myself be loving, kind, and nourishing." Then, state an intention for the evening ahead, such as: "May the words I use tonight, as I talk with my (date, friend, husband), be full of love and kindness. May the conversation we share bring us closer together."

6. Toward the end of your shower, take a few really deep breaths, saying "Ahhhhhh" as you exhale.

7. Stay focused on sensations. When you get out of the shower, notice the texture of the towel you use to dry yourself. Notice how it absorbs the water, how clean your dry skin feels against the towel.

8. Notice your beauty. As you look in the mirror, remember your promise to use kind, loving, and nourishing words when you speak about yourself (and others). Notice the blush in your skin, the color of your eyes . . . really notice. If you look closely, there may be little dancing flecks of blue or gold in your eyes. Admire your beauty and feel grateful for your blessings.

9. Show appreciation for your body. Use your favorite lotion (and a little sweet almond oil added in, if you have some) to gently massage your body. Massage your feet, your legs, your belly, your breasts, your arms, your throat, your face, and finally, your hands. Say a prayer of thankfulness for your body.

A Prayer of Love

A prayer of love can be done in your sacred place, or really in any place that's quiet. You can either sit or stand, as long as you're able to lengthen your spine.

When you are ready, take a few deep breaths, close your eyes, and quiet your mind. Think about when you first met your dinner companion. If it's a new date, think about the thrill of attraction and interest. If it's a friend, remember times you've laughed together. If it's your partner, think about the day you moved in together or your wedding day.

Breathe in as you open your heart center (by raising your shoulders up by your ears, and then lowering them down and back, gently pressing your shoulder blades closer to each other). Exhale, holding an image of your companion in your heart as you say these words:

"May my heart be open to receive you and to connect with your heart.

"May my eyes see you with a childlike delight.

"May we enjoy each other's company, tonight and every night."

Hold thoughts of love and light as you take a few more deep breaths . . . then go get ready to enjoy your night.

Remember that it's important for you to give yourself permission to enjoy a dinner out with other adults, separate from the kids. Moms can take their responsibilities way too seriously; they need to also realize that a happy mom leads to happy children, while an unhappy mom brings negativity and a whole host of other negative emotions to the dinner table.

Mindful Mom

Before you leave for your dinner, spend five minutes sitting quietly with your children (including your teenagers, who will appreciate it even if they roll their eyes). It's not about asking permission; it's about connecting with them to let them know that you are going out to enjoy your companion's company, not to get away from them. Ask them what they've got planned for the evening, and suggest something that might be fun for them to do with the babysitter, such as watch a special video, make popcorn, or work on crafts. Give your children a goodnight kiss, and tell them that you love them. All too often we rush out the door, when stopping for a brief second to connect would lead to the kind of warm, loving feelings that make a world of difference.

INVITE FRIENDS OVER FOR DINNER

"Funny you mention my dinner parties when I have just suggested that inviting close friends over to share a meal with candlelight and wine at your table could be a form of religious experience for some people: To me it's a form of sacrament."

—SALLY QUINN

You've had a tough week, one involving a lot of frustration and little pleasure (unless you've been faithfully doing your meditations). Your cupboard is bare, and you feel the need for a glass of red wine and company. So why not invite friends over for dinner? They've seen your house cluttered, rumpled, and dusty, and they only live five houses down. Get on the cell, and see if they'd like to pool resources and come up with something edible—or better yet, join you for Chinese takeout.

For these occasions, no matter what you eat, set the table and make it an occasion. Light candles, put flowers in a centerpiece, bring out the good wine glasses, and act as if you're eating filet mignon or lobster. This way you'll all feel special, which is guaranteed to boost your spirits.

Since the beginning of history, there are stories of people gathering to break bread, share a meal, and thank God for special blessings.

Before your guests arrive, light a candle and put it on the dinner table, and then take about five minutes to do a simple meditation.

1. Make sure the candle is directly in front of you, at eye level if possible.

2. Close your eyes, and sit at the table with your spine lengthened. It is nice to sit at the very edge of the chair with your feet planted firmly on the floor. That way, you won't be tempted to lean back on the chair.

3. Open your eyes, and gaze at the candle flame for about one minute. Bring all of your concentration to just the candle flame and nothing else. All awareness is in the flame.

4. Notice how the flame jumps around with just a hint of a breeze. Notice the colors of the flame . . . how it is blue at the base and yellow, red, and white on the top. See how the colors change. If your mind begins to chatter or if you get distracted, bring your awareness back to the flame. See it with a child's eye, as though for the first time.

5. Now try to close your eyes but in your mind's eye keep looking at the flame. If you forget exactly how it looks, open your eyes for a second and then close them again. Stay with this candle meditation for about five minutes.

6. When five minutes are almost over, think about who is coming for dinner. Consider a toast for your guests—a toast of gratitude for friendship, for the meal you are serving, and for good health.

7. When your guests show up, stop everything you are doing and greet them at the door. Give each of your guests a really big hug, bringing your hands onto the back of their heart centers. Even if you are not a hugger, you will be offering an amazing gift to your guests.

SUNDAY MEDITATIONS: PREPARE FOR A CALM, COLLECTED WEEK TO COME

"How we think, how we look at our lives, is all-important, and the degree of love we manifest determines the degree of spaciousness and freedom we can bring to life events."

—SHARON SALZBERG

We moms are always trying to finish the world, too. But there is no finishing—and even if we've managed to sneak in some rest on Sunday morning, by late afternoon the demands of the coming week are beginning to weigh on us. By nightfall we can feel completely overwhelmed by the challenges of a week that hasn't even begun yet.

Don't give in to tomorrow's worries today. It's still the day of rest, even for moms. Rather than hurling yourself headlong into the next week, *relax* into it with a special Sunday meditation.

So put your weekly planner aside, and embrace this perfect opportunity to rest, revitalize, and renew. These fifteen minutes—you *do* have fifteen minutes for yourself!—will help you set your intention to remain serene in the face of stress, no matter what the days ahead may bring.

Legs Up the Wall Meditation

Not only is putting your legs up the wall great for circulation, it will also relax you when you are agitated and stressed—perfect for a Sunday night stress-relief session. It takes so little effort!

1. Find a quiet place in your home, and bring a blanket and a pillow with you.

2. Begin by sitting up straight with your right hip against the wall.

3. Bend your knees, and swivel around until you get your legs up the wall. Your butt should be touching the wall. Your body and legs should form a right angle.

4. Once you are in position, to achieve the natural curve of your back, lift your hips, and put a soft pillow under them, nestling it into the small of your back. You want a gentle lift of your hips, with your tailbone spilling over the pillow toward the wall. You may want to put a small folded blanket or rolled up towel behind your neck to lengthen your neck and allow your chin to be at the same height as your forehead. This should feel comfortable and natural.

5. When you are settled into the pose, you can begin the meditation, bringing awareness to all of your bodies—physical, emotional, mental, and spiritual:

   • Scan your physical body, from the crown of your head to your toes. Bring your awareness to the top of your head, and notice every sensation there. Then bring awareness to your face and to all of the muscles around your eyes, jaw, neck, shoulders, and arms, all the way to your fingertips. Work your way slowly down the back and the front of your body—chest, belly, pelvic floor—always resting for a few breaths in each body part and acknowledging any feeling that may be present in each one. Work your way down from your hips, legs, and knees to your ankles, feet, and toes. Imagine that you divide your body in half.

Notice just the right side, and then notice just the left side. Take a moment to reflect on the differences you feel in each body part.

- Next, move to your emotional body. Notice any emotions that may be present. Are you anxious about the coming week? Are you still happy after meeting your friends for a quick brunch? Is there a feeling you've been reluctant to acknowledge, even to yourself? Really take the time to look at each emotion and bring awareness to it.

- Scan your mental body. Notice thoughts, images, chatter, or whatever is present at the moment. Your mental body may be very busy, even midmeditation. Just notice what kind of chattering is going on. Are you making lists, planning, going over a past conversation, or reliving a past experience? Don't linger on any one thought too long. Just notice and be aware.

- Finally, bring awareness to your spiritual body. Does your spirit feel light or burdened? Do you feel any connection to your spirit? To a spiritual force of the universe? Don't make any judgments; just notice.

6. Use your breath and visualize letting go all of this with your exhale. Inhale and feel your breath filling your lungs, and exhale everything out. Give yourself a few minutes to continue to "watch" your breath. With every exhale, let something go. You may be letting go of a tight hip or of a feeling of sadness. Once you feel that a lot has been let go of, just enjoy the sensation of your breath. Stay as long as you are able to for your "Sunday Meditation Time."

7. When you are ready, bend your knees and roll to one side. Stay there for a few breaths, and then press yourself up and stay seated for a few breaths. When you are ready, come to a standing position, wrap your arms around yourself and give yourself a hug, and have a wonderful day.

Simple Legs Up the Wall

If the legs up the wall meditation seems too complicated, just focus on your breath in the pose. Bring your hands to your belly, and feel the rise and fall of your breath, like a wave on a calm day. As you inhale, the wave is going out to sea, and as you exhale, the wave is coming to shore. With eyes closed, consider your connection to the sea; you are, after all, made up of as much as 75 percent water!

Double-Duty Serenity

You don't have to reserve this legs up the wall meditation just for Sunday nights. Do it any time that you feel you are running ragged. Give your legs—and the rest of your body, mind, and soul—a break. Kids love this one, too; so if they're exhausted and overstimulated, have them join you. Don't be surprised if they settle down for a nap afterward; this is a pose beloved by insomniacs for its ability to induce sleep.

LAST-RESORT MEDITATIONS

"When you begin to touch your heart or let your heart be touched, you begin to discover that it's bottomless, that it doesn't have any resolution, that this heart is huge, vast, and limitless. You begin to discover how much warmth and gentleness is there, as well as how much space."

—PEMA CHÖDRÖN

As a mom, you are continually bombarded with demands on your time. These demands can be physical, emotional, mental, or spiritual, and it's easy to be completely overwhelmed in all of these bodies. In order to bring more awareness to everything happening in your world, you need to come more fully into each of your bodies.

Watching the Breath

This exercise is sometimes called *Shamatha with support.* Shamatha means calm abiding, tranquility, or meditation. All we are doing is watching breathing—no more, no less. This breath watching will, with even a few minutes, calm the nervous system and bring a feeling of peace. With the breath, this peace can come very easily and naturally.

Close your eyes. Close your mouth. Take a few minutes to pay attention to your breath:

- **Notice the length of each in-breath.** If your in-breaths are only two or three seconds long, they are shallow breaths, a surefire sign that you're stressed.
- **Notice the temperature of the breath.** Is it cool when you inhale and warm when you exhale?
- **Notice the direction of the breath.** When you inhale, can you feel the breath filling your lungs and causing your belly to expand? Can you feel the breath entering your nose and cooling the inside and then passing downward into your lungs?

After bringing all this awareness to the breath as it is, slowly begin to inhale longer and deeper. You want each in-breath to be about five or six seconds long and the exhale to be an equal length of time.

Bring your right hand to your belly. Breathe deeply (five or six seconds), drawing in air until your belly presses into your hand. As you exhale, let your navel sink until it is pressing toward your spine.

Continue breathing in and out as you begin to count the breath: 1, 2, 3, 4, 5 for the in-breath and 5, 4, 3, 2, 1 for the exhale. If counting seems too boring, say a mantra, such as "May I have peace" as you inhale and "May all have peace" as you exhale.

Simple Watching the Breath

If you're feeling super stressed, you can simplify this even further. If this exercise is *really* a last resort, just sit (or lie down), bring your hand to your belly, and count to five on the inhale and count to five on the exhale. Do this for a few minutes, and notice how the simple act of breathing can calm your emotions.

CHAPTER SUMMARY

Ah, weekends, those bastions of relaxation . . . just kidding! But hopefully you've gained insight into ways you can simplify your life enough to enjoy your weekends far more than you have in the past. So what did you learn? To sum it up:

- Before rushing off to run errands, it really pays to get in tune with your higher self and pare down that list to what's essential.
- Slowing down normal activities, such as eating, helps you learn how to stay mindfully in the moment, which will help you get in touch with your intuition (which often gets drowned out by the noise and commotion around you).
- Rewarding yourself for running errands that you hate is a marvelous form of motivation—that works!
- Pausing to create prayerful intentions for your day will help your mind focus on what's important.
- Humming in the shower lets your family know you're happy and offers a way for you to choose your words carefully when it matters.
- Inviting friends over for dinner is a treat for all!
- Sunday nights bring their own challenges, but yoga offers amazing meditations that will have you leaping out of bed the next morning, raring to go.

Of course, weekends also bring sports and hobbies into the picture. Everyone has something they want to do, even Mom. Turn the page, and we'll offer strategies for keeping everyone happy—especially you!

7

Sports and Hobbies

*"Sport strips away personality, letting the white bone
of character shine through. Sport gives players an
opportunity to know and test themselves."*

—RITA MAE BROWN

All of us have something that we love to do, and part of mothering is noticing what activities stir passion in your children's hearts and helping them find ways to participate. Some children will be athletically inclined, gravitating quite naturally to competitive sports or individual challenges such as ice skating, skateboarding, swimming, and so on. Some will favor artistic endeavors such as music, art, or crafts. Some may favor academic activities like science camp or mathletes. Whatever their predilections and enthusiasms bring, you will likely have active children who will be begging for opportunities to do what they love.

Maybe you have childhood memories that are driving you to push your children into as many activities as possible—or quite the opposite; maybe you felt forced into activities that you hated and want to give your children free rein. Either way, it's wise to grapple with these decisions, ferreting out your feelings—and theirs. You can begin, of course, by asking your child what she really loves to do, exploring options together, and then paring them down to the top priorities. Your children won't suffer if you pare down activities, focusing on the most important ones while letting some slide. In fact, the simpler you keep your life, the better chance you have of fulfilling your needs—and theirs.

MEDITATIONS FOR DEALING WITH CONFLICTS

"There are two ways of meeting difficulties: You alter the difficulties or you alter yourself meeting them."

—PHYLLIS BOTTOME

Having your family involved in sports and hobbies means not only setting priorities but also dealing with conflicts that arise because of their participation. For example, when one child's important soccer game is on the same day as the other's science fair, which do you attend? When the coach is playing favorites, or the other parents set your teeth on edge, conflict brews. Remember to be mindful when dealing with these difficulties. Here's a loving kindness meditation that is a good way to center yourself before dealing with conflicts and decisions you must make.

Metta (Loving Kindness) Meditation

Metta meditation is considered priceless and a treasure to help bring intimacy with ourselves first and then with others. The Buddha was precise about the benefits of this meditation and proclaimed that:

1. You will sleep easily.
2. You will wake easily.
3. You will have pleasant dreams.
4. People will love you.
5. Devas (celestial beings) and animals will love you.
6. Devas will protect you.
7. Poisons, weapons, and fire (external dangers) will not harm you.
8. Your face will be radiant.
9. Your mind will be serene.
10. You will die unconfused.
11. You will be reborn in happy realms.

To begin, come to a quiet place, and breathe slowly, until you begin to feel calm.

State this wish for yourself: "May I be happy and free from suffering." As you say these words to yourself, acknowledge all of your goodness.

Next, think of someone you have a strong respect and gratitude for, and visualize him (or her) as you state this wish: "May Jonathan be happy and free from suffering."

Next, think of a close friend and say: "May Paula be happy and free from suffering."

Next, think of a neutral person, someone whom you do not know very well, such as someone who may work at a coffee shop or the UPS person, and state: "May my UPS delivery person be happy and free from suffering."

Next, think of a difficult person, someone whom you do not like, and state: "May Harold be happy and free from suffering." This can be challenging. Maybe bring that person to mind and linger for a while, thinking about others whom you also do not like.

End the Metta meditation by thinking of *all beings*, and state: "May all beings be happy and free from suffering."

Do not force or even try to manufacture disingenuous feelings of any kind, such as feelings of love for someone whom you do not like. Just say the words as though the words were delicate glass sculptures, and in doing so, you may feel more loving toward that person and toward *all beings*.

This meditation can be taught to children and can be done together in the car. If a child has a teacher or coach whom they do not like, this would be a great practice.

Here's a meditation to release stress, which you may need after a hectic Saturday of ferrying children to games and events.

Tennis Ball Meditation with TV

This exercise will help you release those knots of stress that you may be keeping in your back. Find a tennis ball that is used and just a little flat. Keep this tennis ball handy as you begin.

1. Turn on a mindless TV show, and lie down on a rug or your yoga mat.

2. Use your right hand to place the tennis ball under your back, between your spine and your left shoulder blade.
3. Bend your left knee, placing your foot up close to your bottom.
4. Inhale, and release your hands down by your sides.
5. Exhale, and let the weight of your body slowly come down onto the tennis ball.
6. Press into your left foot to roll your back a few inches up and down over the ball. Notice the valley of knots! The tennis ball is staying on the side of the spine.
7. Find your most tender knot, and allow your body to sink over the ball. Say (or moan) "Ohhhhh."
8. Breathe deeply. If this is too intense, put a towel between you and the tennis ball. If you want to intensify this exercise, straighten your bent leg.
9. Do the other side.

A Variation

While still lying down, put the tennis ball under your right buttock, and roll it around until you find the perfect knot. You may have lots of knots. Find your "favorite" knot (the one that's always there), and let your buttock sink down onto the tennis ball. Find another knot, and do the same. Stay for as long as you like, gently rolling, and then do the other side.

When your work is complete, enjoy the feeling of lightness. You may feel like you can levitate.

Relaxation Meditation

Now that you've worked out the kinks in your back, try this simple meditation to calm your mind.

Simply follow the breath and anchor it to a word or phrase.

Inhale and say "Peace."

Exhale and say "Relax."

Inhale . . . "Peace."

Exhale . . . "Relax."

Have no agenda—just the breath.

This seems almost too simple, but the results can be significant in terms of releasing stress, slowing down, and centering yourself.

Me-Time: Make Time for Your Sport

When you're working out the schedule, make sure you pencil in time for participating in whatever sport *you* love, whether it's working out at the gym, bicycling around the lake, tennis matches with your best friend, mountain climbing, or jogging through the grocery store. The point is that your physical pleasure matters as much as anyone else's, and it won't happen if you don't make it a priority.

THE SPORTING LIFE

*"The ability to laugh at yourself
is a sign of mental health."*

—JUDITH HANSON

Sports are fun for kids, but they're a whole lot of work for mom. You'll likely be the person in charge, the one who makes sure that your children sign up for their chosen sports and who handles all that comes with sports, such as buying whatever equipment they need, scheduling days to make sure everyone gets where they're supposed to be, and carpooling them to practices, games, and after-game parties. You'll also be the one cheering loudest, wiping their tears when they lose, and tucking those tired little athletes into bed at night. Yes, sports present a challenge, but we know you're up to the task.

Among the challenges is that playing sports usually leads to your child's introduction to competition, which can come as quite a surprise to someone who has been shielded. They'll need help learning how to play on a team, which offers more "teachable moments" than you thought would ever come your way—particularly when you factor in learning how to recognize and cope with pregame anxiety and learning how to be a loser and a winner. Even if it's not a competitive sport, your child will be learning a lot about himself, which means you'll need to keep an even keel so you can help him navigate those waters.

Mindful Mom

Playing games with young children is an ideal way to teach them how to be thoughtful even while being competitive. Through conscious modeling, you can show them the joys of playing with others, how to build their own levels of confidence without diminishing anyone else's feelings, and the highs and lows of winning and losing. Plus, playing games with your children is something they thoroughly enjoy, and you might as well enjoy it while they're young, before playing with mom is not so cool.

Dealing with Anxiety

If you're lucky, you've got an extremely secure child who doesn't get worked up before games or competitions. On the other hand, if you have a sensitive child, whose anxiety builds in the days and hours leading up to the big event, the sooner you address his spoken, and often unspoken, anxiety, the happier you'll all be. After you've given him all the reasons why this should be fun and why the end result doesn't matter, try a visualization exercise to quell his worries. After all, if anyone knows about pressure, it's you!

Roaring Lion Meditation

If feelings are too pent-up to move on, mimicking a roaring lion should do the trick:

- Sit on your heels, bring your hands onto your knees, open your fingers like the claws of a lion, and lean forward.
- Open your mouth as wide as you can, stick out your tongue as far as you can, and open your eyes as wide as you can.
- Inhale, and as you exhale, roar as long and as loud as you can. Keep roaring until all the bad feelings have dissipated.

This pose relaxes your face and neck, which helps release a clenched jaw.

WINNERS AND LOSERS

"Not knowing when the down will come,
I open every door."

—EMILY DICKINSON

Everyone loves to win and hates to lose, and we all need to know how to handle both with grace and dignity. One way to smooth any untoward emotions that your children may experience when they lose is to do a meditation with them in which they focus on the winner qualities we all possess. This way, they'll get in touch with their inner winner, even if on a losing team.

Warrior Pose

To begin, you can tell your children that a true warrior has strength and wisdom and a strong heart. A warrior celebrates another's victory with generosity. It's not about who wins; it's about being strong enough to compete with honor and both win and lose gracefully. It's about honoring your opponents and yourself—win, lose, or draw. Then, teach them the warrior pose:

1. Start with your feet hip-width apart.
2. Inhale, and place your hands on your hips.
3. Exhale, step your left foot back, bend your right knee and allow your body to sink down through your sitting bones. Press back through the heel of your left foot.
4. Inhale, and raise your arms upward, bringing them perpendicular to the floor and parallel to one another. Reach your arms as high as you can to stretch your ribcage. While continuing to breathe, hold this pose for 30 to 60 seconds.
5. To release, lean forward and bring your left foot back to meet the right. And bring your hands back to your hips.
6. Take a few breaths, and then do the other side.

Remember to Breathe

Another useful skill to teach your children is how to breathe when they feel anxious or upset. Breath of joy is a simple breathing exercise you can teach your kids to help them lighten the mood and restore their upbeat attitude.

Breath of Joy

This pose will actually bring a smile to your face and to your child's face. Once your child smiles, his anxiety will lower. A happy child equals a happy mother!

1. Stand with your feet about one foot apart, with your knees softly bent.
2. Inhale as you raise your arms in front of you to shoulder height . . . inhale some more, opening your arms out to the sides . . . inhale even more, raising your arms overhead, and then exhale, saying "HA!" as you swing your arms down toward the ground, bending forward from the hips.
3. Use momentum to swing your arms back up to shoulder height as you bring your body upright, and repeat as many times as you would like.
4. Keep going and begin to pick up the speed. With each "HA!," make it louder and louder. You will find yourself and your kids smiling and eventually even laughing.

MAKE THE MOST OF YOUR TIME

"Other people may not have had high expectations for me . . . but I had high expectations for myself."

—SHANNON MILLER

As we've said before, having active kids means you'll spend an inordinate amount of time either waiting around or watching various events. Here are more ways to make the most of your time by getting in a little meditation.

Yin Practice

An entire yin practice can be done while sitting on a chair or bleacher bench. Yin yoga is a passive posture that you hold for several minutes. The purpose of each posture is to get into the connective tissues of the body, to tug and tax the tissues to create suppleness. Most injuries in athletes are not injuries to the muscles but are caused by injuries in the joints; creating suppleness in the joints helps prevent injuries. Yin postures work by relaxing the muscles and strengthening and lubricating the connective tissues in the joints. Once the joint is lubricated, it is less apt to be damaged.

Each yin posture stimulates a different set of meridians (energy channels) that run throughout the body and that stimulate and balance specific organ functions. Each organ is related to a particular emotion. As busy mothers, we may become out of balance from all kinds of things: stress, exhaustion, multitasking, and so on. When we are out of balance in our kidneys, the emotional flavor is fear; the spleen, worry or obsession; the liver, anger; the lungs, sadness and grief; and the heart, depression and hatred.

You can use these yin postures as an opportunity to investigate what's happening now. Look at the emotion with curiosity, and let it go. Emotions are sometimes held in our bodies for years. Yoga postures and meditations can help release these stored emotions to bring a lightness to your overall being.

You may want to invite another parent to join you in your meditative yin postures. When you're at a practice, or the actual sporting event, sit on a folded chair or in the bleachers, and take a few falling-out breaths. Remember: these are breaths that you inhale through your nose and exhale through your mouth, saying "Haaaaaa." After a few falling-out breaths, just breathe in and out of your nose if you are able.

Fold Over Pose

Cross your right ankle over your left knee.

Feel both of your hip bones pressing down evenly on the seat.

Inhale, filling up your lungs. As you exhale, fold forward until you feel your right hip and buttocks release and open up. (You can still be watching the game.) Place your arms on the inside of the calf of your right leg, folding one palm over the other. Let your back relax into the fold. You want to be at an edge, meaning that you want to feel this strongly but not painfully. The point just before pain begins is a good strong edge.

Once you feel your edge, commit to staying still for at least three minutes, and as many as seven. During this long hold, try to relax all of your muscles and let the tug be deep inside your joints. Breathe evenly. If you are holding your breath or gasping, you are too deep into the stretch and need to back off. If you are at a practice and you do not feel you need to watch, let your eyes close and become aware of all of your physical, emotional, and mental sensations.

Do not judge what may come up for you. Just notice with curiosity, and let the sensation go.

After a few minutes, switch sides. In our culture, we tend to hold a lot of tension in our hips (and shoulders), creating tightness in our lower backs. When you open your hips in this posture, it will also open your lower back. This posture will stimulate the liver meridian.

Twisting Pose

This spinal twist stimulates your kidney meridian. If your kidneys are out of balance, you may experience feeling fearful when nothing is genuinely creating fear.

1. Sit up tall in your chair or on the bleacher bench. Sitting at the edge will help lengthen your spine. Bring your chin slightly toward your chest to lengthen your neck.
2. Do a few falling-out breaths. Inhale deeply, and exhale saying "Haaaa."
3. Begin to breathe in and out of your nose, slowly and deeply.
4. Inhale. As you exhale, bring your left hand over to your right knee, draping it around your knee, if comfortably possible.

5. Turn your head to gaze over your right shoulder.
6. Bring your right hand behind you, and press down on the seat for leverage to help you to keep your spine erect.
7. Stay for a few minutes, and then switch sides.

Folding Over Pose

Doing this exercise, you will get a great stretch in your lower back, which will stimulate your kidney meridians. When out of balance, the kidney meridians hold obsession and worry. When you are up at night and cannot sleep because your mind is racing in circles, this could be an imbalance in the kidneys. This exercise will help rebalance you.

1. Sit at the edge of your chair or bleacher bench.
2. Open your knees about one foot.
3. Sit upright, and do a few falling-out breaths. Inhale through you nose, and exhale through your mouth, saying "Haaaa."
4. Inhale again. When you exhale, reach your arms forward and all the way to the ground, bending at your waist.
5. Let the tops of your hands press the surface at your feet. Stretch as far as you can, and stay for a few minutes. If you are able to do so comfortably, breathe in and out through your nose; if not, breathe through your mouth.
6. Notice where you feel this stretch, and use this focus to consciously release the worries creating the muscle tension.

Straight-Leg Forward Bend

This pose is also good for the kidneys and for releasing worry.

1. Sit up straight on the edge of your chair or bleacher bench.
2. Do a few falling-out breaths. Inhale through the nose, and exhale, saying "Haaaa."
3. Breathe deeply through your nose, or through your mouth if that's not comfortable.
4. Straighten your legs in front of you, and flex your feet by pressing your toes toward your forehead; feel your hamstrings stretch.
5. Lean forward without bending your knees. Come to your edge, that point just before pain begins, and stay for a few minutes.

    You can stay with this stretch while watching your child; or if you are at a practice and don't need to watch, or while your child is taking a break, try closing your eyes.
6. Notice any physical, emotional, or mental experiences you may be having, such as a tight hamstring, or feeling overwhelmed, or worrying about something happening in your workplace. Each time a thought or emotion surfaces, try to replace it with a breath. Or you can envision a stream and picture each thought or sensation or emotion as a leaf floating by. For example, you may be in your posture and realize that you are planning dinner in your head. Look at this thought, and let it float by. You may be in a posture and begin reliving a quarrel you had with a family member. Notice this, thinking "*Oh, rather than attaching to this quarrel, I'm going to let it float down the river.*" This leaf floating of

sensations and thoughts becomes a mindfulness meditation. Some people also picture troubling thoughts or emotions as butterflies that flit easily into the atmosphere.

Some days you may find that you are not able to use this technique to release thoughts or sensations, which is fine. Learning to release your need to succeed is called *acceptance*. You will have days when this works and other days when it just does not. With practice, it will become easier to let the leaf float downstream.

Back Bend

This back-bending pose has you arching in the upper back, which helps you stimulate your heart and lung meridians. This set of meridians may bring up feelings of sadness and grief, depression and hatred. By bringing them up, you can also let them go. If you find the feelings too overwhelming to experience at a sporting event, then come out of the pose and try it again at another time when you have privacy and space.

1. Sit at the edge of your chair or bleacher bench.
2. Do a few falling-out breaths. Inhale through your nose, and exhale, saying "Haaaa."
3. Inhale and reach your arms forward, clasping your hands and interlacing your fingers.
4. With your fingers interlaced, turn your palms away from you.
5. Round your spine and bring your chin to your chest.

6. Exhale and reach upward. Look up (but do not crunch the back of your neck).

7. Arch your back. Think of your heart center reaching forward and lifting upward. In other words, you are arching more in the upper back than anywhere else.

8. Reach as far as you can, and stay for a couple of minutes.

9. Come forward again, rounding your spine like a cat arching its back.

10. Do this a few times.

Always come slowly out of any back bend, and then round your spine to release any tension.

Hug Your Knees Posture

In addition to stimulating your heart and lung meridians, this pose is great for digestion, as it gives your lower organs a gentle massage.

1. Sit upright, bring your knees toward your chest, and wrap your arms around your knees. Keep your shoulders and chin down.

2. Your feet are up off the ground, and you're balancing on your bottom.

3. As you inhale, let your belly press into your quads and as you exhale, bring your navel in toward your spine. Stay for a few minutes, just focusing on your breath.

When you have completed the physical portion and returned to a sitting position, briefly bring to mind worries or problems or emotions that may be tying up your digestive process, and then quickly and consciously release them.

MEDITATIVE HOBBIES

"Learning how to be kind to ourselves, learning how to respect ourselves, is important. The reason it's important is that, fundamentally, when we look into our own hearts and begin to discover what is confused and what is brilliant, what is bitter and what is sweet, it isn't just ourselves that we're discovering. We're discovering the universe."

—PEMA CHÖDRÖN

You should always make time for a hobby or two. Hobbies are great for everyone, but especially for you! One great thing about hobbies is that they offer marvelous opportunities to quiet your mind. They also allow you to be creative, to produce something beautiful or meaningful—perhaps using your hands, which always feels good. Hobbies also provide occasions for you to teach your kids all sorts of skills and to interact with them in a restful, playful manner. The choice of hobbies is endless, but we've come up with some that offer unique opportunities to be creative and meditative, two things that will nourish your soul and make you be a happier mom.

Photo Collages

If you have a scanner, you can scan family pictures and combine them with pictures you pull from magazines to create collages. Each of you can create your own storyboard, arranging pictures in a way that reveals who you are and what's important to you. It's an ideal time to spark conversations with your children that will help them learn to know themselves better . . . and it might just do the same for you.

Make this hobby mindful by reflecting on what the art says about where your heart is. If the collage shows things that you aspire to have or be, consider why you're not making them part of your life now.

Map Your Family Tree

Tracing your genealogy is another great way to engage your children in learning more about who they are and how they fit in the world. As you fill in the information about grandparents and great-grandparents, you can tell your children any stories you've heard about your ancestors. Soon everyone will be laughing, and the memories you shared and the ones you've created will stay with them. Tell as many funny stories as you can; to reinforce what they've learned, talk about the stories in the coming weeks. Great family stories can also make great bedtime stories.

To make this a mindful hobby, think about each of your family members and what makes you grateful about them—even the ones who drive you nuts! What is a good thing about that person, something you can appreciate and admire? Share your thoughts with your children to make it a family moment of gratefulness.

Me-Time: Artist's Date

One way to nourish your creativity is to make artist's dates. All this means is that you spend a few hours, or an entire afternoon (if you have that luxury), doing something that stimulates your creativity. It could be a trip to gallery, two hours alone with your journal and a set of colored pencils, a walk in nature, an afternoon at a local garden club photographing flowers, meeting a friend who shares your passion for reading, shopping for yarn, or going to see a movie alone—whatever helps you reconnect with your inner artist and celebrate your creativity. The best part: goals are not encouraged. It's all about process, and recognizing what springs forth when you honor whatever it is in you that seeks creative expression. Enjoy!

Create a Treasure Map

This one's great fun for everyone! The kids will love hiding "treasures" and then creating treasure maps for each other to follow. It can generate conversation about what is a treasure to them and why. And while they are excitedly drawing their own maps, you can spend time creating a treasure map of your own, one that maps out what you want to happen next in your life. Allow yourself to approach it playfully; you'll soon be flooded with ideas, and all you'll have to do is follow the yellow-brick road.

If you need a little help making ideas flow, try the following meditation.

Stirring the Pot Meditation

Sit on the floor or a yoga mat. If it would feel more comfortable, place a folded blanket or small pillow under your hips. Cross your legs, and bring your hands down onto your knees. Pretend you are sitting on a big clock.

1. Lean over toward your right knee, and circle your upper body over toward your left knee. Continue circling around until you make a big circle going in a counterclockwise direction.
2. Inhale as you round forward, gently sticking out your chin.
3. Then, exhale as you round back, bringing your chin toward your chest.
4. As you are "stirring the pot," think back in your past. You are going counterclockwise! Think about something that hasn't worked out for you. Can you let this memory go?
5. Keep going around for a few minutes. What else comes up for you in your past?
6. Now reverse directions, and this time close your eyes and look up toward your third-eye point (the place between and above your eyebrows). Think about what you would like to see in your future.

7. As you continue rotating in a clockwise direction, pretend you have a great big canvas and you are going to create a work of art. This work of art will embody what your heart's desire is. Take as long as you want creating this imaginary canvas. You can use imaginary paint, pen, photos, or anything that your creative imagination can come up with!

8. After you are finished creating a vision of your heart's desire, stop and "study" it with your eyes closed. What do you see? What is your third eye "telling" you?

9. When you feel ready, slowly open your eyes, retaining a clear memory of what your heart most wants to have happen.

This is a great time to journal about what you have created. If you can clearly see it and visualize it coming true, it is more apt to become a reality.

CLAIM YOUR CREATIVITY

"Adults are always asking little kids
what they want to be when they grow up
because they're looking for ideas."

—PAULA POUNDSTONE

If you're having trouble reawakening your creativity, you might want to stimulate your second chakra. Your second chakra (remember: a chakra is a wheel of energy) lies in your pelvic region, where your reproductive organs are located. It has to do with desire and sensual pleasures, but also with change and creativity. We usually think that only artists are truly creative, but that is incorrect. Everyone has the gift of creativity. If we can learn to let go of the results, we can really unleash our creativity and enjoy expressing ourselves.

As a mother you can do anything creatively; sorting your underwear drawer can be done creatively. How you cut your child's sandwich or arrange the groceries in your pantry can be done with a creative energy. How about writing a children's book, with no desire to have it published? It is the process that can be enjoyed. Remember how you used to love to color and paint when you were a child? When did you stop? How about using finger paints and crayons to literally create your own masterpiece?

Stimulate Your Second Chakra

Opening and stimulating your second chakra will help you renew your creative energy. This is great if you are in the middle of a project and have lost your creative energy or if you just want to start a project with a creative intent.

Pelvic Tilt

1. Stand with your feet slightly more than hip-width apart, keeping your knees slightly bent.
2. Bring your hands to your knees.
3. Exhale as you round your spine, bringing your chin to your chest. Tilt the bottom of your pelvis forward.
4. Inhale as you reverse this position. Arch your back, look up, and stick your chest out.
5. Continue tilting and arching for about three minutes.

When you feel ready, proceed to working on your creative project, feeling as if you have literally primed your creative pump (because you have!).

Make Cleanup Fun

The most wonderful part of art projects is that they are incredibly fun, and the worst part about art projects is that they can create a total mess. So, rather than getting upset about spilled glue, or glitter over every single piece of furniture in the room, why not make cleanup a game, or sing a silly song together? Try the cleanup song:

"Clean up, clean up, everybody, everywhere.

"Clean up, clean up, everybody do your share."

Or, you can make the cleanup process an act of mindfulness. Pay careful attention to what you're doing: the way the broom feels in your hands as you sweep up, the pleasing row of colors from the bottles of paint as you put them back on the shelf, the twinkle of the spilled glitter, or the satisfaction of getting the spilled glue to come up.

LAST-RESORT MEDITATION

"Often we can achieve an even better result when we stumble yet are willing to start over, when we don't give up after a mistake, when something doesn't come easily but we throw ourselves into trying, when we're not afraid to appear less than perfectly polished."

—SHARON SALZBERG

If your children have played their sport or enjoyed their hobbies but you haven't squeezed out a single minute for yourself, you may feel a little stressed. While witnessing your children's smiles and feeling their happiness is rewarding in and of itself, you've ended up feeling left out. Once again, you've put everyone's needs above your own, telling yourself that it really doesn't matter—but it does. There's a small girl inside you who feels like she's not important. She may even hold resentment about what she gave up to become a mother and how she is constantly being asked to wait at the end of the line when it comes to pleasure. Rather than brush these feelings aside, you need to give your inner child her due. Try this meditation to reconnect with her.

Two Ways to Honor Your Inner Child

For the first meditation, find a quiet place to sit, and close your eyes.

1. Breathe slowly until you begin to feel calm. (Never worry if you are not able to get to a calm place. That will come with time and practice.)
2. Think back to when you were a child. Try to remember a time when you were not feeling acknowledged or loved. See if you can remember the circumstances and what led to those feelings. Try to see yourself as a child in the memory. Embody the memory by remembering little details, like what you were wearing, or what time of year it was, or who else was present.
3. During this process, keep your breath long and even, returning focus to your breath as needed. If the memory is really difficult or painful, you can choose not to go there and try another memory.
4. With your eyes remaining closed, "look" into the eyes of the child (that was you) and visualize wrapping your arms around her and talking softly with her. If she is crying, let her continue to cry while you hold her. If you begin to cry, let the tears flow.

5. When you both feel more composed, gently ask your inner child to tell you why she feels left out or unloved. Listen intently, allowing her feelings to wash over you.

6. When the story feels complete, tell her you are sorry that she felt this way in the past. Reassure her that you love her and want to make her happy.

7. Say farewell to her, and after a moment of resting in silence, go back to focusing on your breath. Inhale memory . . . exhale acceptance and love.

8. Continue breathing until you feel re-energized.

Another meditation that can help you honor your inner child involves happy memories!

1. Breathe slowly in and out until you feel calm.

2. Think back to when you were a child, to a time when you were feeling good about yourself, and happy.

3. Remember any details, like what you were wearing and who was with you. Why were you feeling so proud or joyful?

4. See yourself as that happy child, and move closer so you can be with her and share the happy moment.

5. Notice how it feels to re-experience childlike joy. Can you bring that feeling into your life right now?

6. Stay with this experience, breathing slowly in and out, until you feel very happy and ready to come out and play!

After you have reconnected with your inner child, you can move on to honoring the woman you have become.

Honor Your Womanhood Meditation

If possible, find a place to sit outside, facing the east (where the sun rises). Otherwise, go to your sacred space inside and sit there. Light a candle. Acknowledge that the east is where each new day is born.

Reach your right arm and fingers toward the east, and bring your left hand onto your left knee with your first finger and thumb touching. (The first finger represents your soul, and the thumb represents the soul of the universe.) This is a mudra that symbolizes your connection to the universe.

Say:

"I am the light of my soul."

"I am bountiful."

"I am beautiful."

"I am bliss."

"I am, I am."

Say each of these affirmations a few times out loud.

Couch Pose

If that doesn't do the trick, maybe you can find one fun thing to do before the day ends. It could be anything, no matter how silly. How about a yoga pose that will amuse your kids and give your energy a badly needed boost?

Couch pose is a supported shoulder stand that's a great rejuvenator. It gives your heart a break from constantly pumping blood all the way down your legs and back up again. It also helps blood rush into your upper body and face.

Please note that you should not do inverted poses if you have high blood pressure or problems with your eyes. Even if you're fine in those areas, always make sure that your neck is fully supported (a folded blanket or pillow can be placed under your shoulders) and always heed any pain. If it hurts, don't do it!

1. Grab a folded blanket or soft pillow and place it on the floor in front of your couch.
2. Sit directly above the blanket, and then swivel your body and swing your legs up onto the back of the couch with your legs straight.
3. Shimmy your hips to the very edge of the couch and raise your hands up and over your head to steady yourself as you slowly lower your head and shoulders toward the floor. Pause to position the folded blanket or pillow under your shoulders, and then slither down until you are resting your head on the floor. Your shoulders and neck should be softly curved and feel fully supported by the folded blanket, while your hips are supported by the edge of the couch.
4. When you feel completely supported, position your arms overhead, as if they were goal posts, elbows softly bent and palms facing up.
5. Stay upside down, breathing, as long as feels comfortable. (The kids will want to join you.)

You will feel marvelous after you come out of this couch pose.

CHAPTER SUMMARY

Sports and hobbies provide a lot of enjoyment, but they also require a lot of planning, time, and dedication. No matter your children's interests, they will have activities that they want to—and need to—participate in. Narrowing down choices and making the most of your time will make this part of your family life flow a little more smoothly. Here's what you learned:

- Accepting that frustrations exist can be helpful, but holding tension in your body is not good. Rolling your back on a cleverly placed simple tennis ball can help you pinpoint and release muscle tension.
- One of the best things you can do for your children is to teach them how to interact with teammates and graciously win and lose. Warrior pose, and the philosophy that goes along with it, is a tool for teaching good sportsmanship.
- Focusing on breath will help calm anxious children so they can get back in the game.
- Making kids laugh can really help lower anxiety. Certain yoga poses are guaranteed to end in peals of laughter.
- You can productively use the time spent waiting for practices and games to end by doing some yin yoga postures.
- Hobbies offer many meditative moments, particularly if they're calming activities.
- Engaging your children in certain hobbies, like mapping family trees and treasure maps, can strengthen family bonds.

- Meditation and yoga can help you reconnect with your natural creativity.
- Your intuition provides a gateway to your creativity.

Who knew having fun could be so exhausting? Thankfully, you've got a vacation coming up. Oh, wait—those can offer a whole new set of challenges. No worries; we're on it!

8

On Vacation

*"By and large, mothers and housewives are the
only workers who do not have regular time off.
They are the great vacation-less class."*

—ANNE MORROW LINDBERGH

It's your first real family vacation in two years. You've all agreed that a week at the beach would be a little slice of heaven, and, after hours of searching, you managed to find a cottage you can actually afford. For weeks you've been talking about the fun that you'll all have enjoying the beach. Everyone excitedly created his or her own fantasy vacation—especially you. As the date approaches, spirits are running high.

Then, after weeks of planning, coordinating, preparing, and packing, you're shoving the suitcases into the trunk, almost ready to go . . . and your son starts fussing because he can't remember if he packed his favorite sweatshirt, your daughter starts whining because she can't find her teddy bear, your baby is crying and running a low-grade fever, and you feel like throwing your hands up in exasperation.

Oh, yes; it's vacation time, when life is supposed to be sweet. You knew getting there would be the hardest part, but you didn't foresee the mayhem that's unfolding. It's enough to make you want to unpack everything and go back to bed . . . only then you'd dream about the fabulous vacations you had as a child and how much you wanted your family to be as happy as clams.

It's time to stop, breathe, and regroup.

COUNT YOUR BREATHS INSTEAD OF YOUR BLESSINGS

"Those who say you can't take it with you never saw a car packed for a vacation."

—AUTHOR UNKNOWN

If you find yourself in this predicament, don't allow feelings to bubble over and get your vacation off on the wrong foot. No matter how much you're looking forward to the vacation, tension can arise. Children can become anxious about leaving their homes, particularly if they don't know where they're going. Moms (and dads) can become a little unnerved by the preparations, pressure, and expense of taking a vacation. And it's supposed to be fun!

If your family is on the brink of a meltdown, stop everything and breathe.

Follow Your Breath Meditation

Count your breaths and your blessings, bringing in peace and exhaling frustration. Breathe in peace, and breathe out frustration. The intention is not to count but to follow the breath. Counting will help you to notice when your mind wanders. If you lose track of what number you are on, you know that your mind has wandered. If you lose your place, start with the number "one" again.

1. Sit quietly and comfortably so you can breathe deeply.
2. Count *one* as you slowly inhale . . . count *two* as you slowly exhale.
3. Count *two* as you slowly inhale, and count *three* as you slowly exhale.
4. Count *three* as you slowly inhale, and count *four* as you slowly exhale.
5. Count *four* as you slowly inhale, and count *five* as you slowly exhale.
6. Count until you get to *ten*, and if you don't feel at peace, start over.

Get the Show on the Road

Now it's time to get the job done. Open your son's suitcase to see if his sweatshirt is packed; find your daughter's teddy bear; and pack some Tylenol for the baby. Reassure yourself and everyone else that all will be fine, and hustle everyone into the car. On the drive, after the kids fall asleep (which they will, and rather quickly), allow your thoughts to settle, and consciously clear away any lingering debris related to what *almost* went awry. Instead, visualize some happy memories of vacations you've taken in the past, and set the intention that this vacation will help you and your children create happy memories.

Reasons to Take a Vacation

Vacations are essential, not only because they offer a break in your everyday routine, but because they offer adventure and opportunities to introduce your children to new experiences. In case you need additional reasons, vacations help you:

- reduce stress; this has immediate, positive effects on your health.
- have enough brain space to reconnect with your inner self and feel more aligned with your purpose in life, what you hope to accomplish.
- come home feeling physically refreshed and ready to take on the world again.
- return mentally rested yet brimming with ideas and enthusiasm.
- sleep better and feel happier, which can last as long as two months after the vacation ends.
- deepen family bonds and create happy memories for all.

So just when you think they're not worth all the fuss, vacations begin to sound heavenly—and they can be, with a little forethought.

FORETHOUGHT SETS THE STAGE

*"I soon realized that no journey carries one far
unless, as it extends into the world around us, it
goes an equal distance into the world within."*

—LILLIAN SMITH

Because vacations provide so many benefits, planning a vacation calls for considerable forethought. By that we mean taking time to consider alternatives and to include everyone in the final decision. Of course you have every right to plan whatever vacation you want to plan, but some vacations are not child friendly, and you'll likely enjoy those vacations much more if you leave the kids at home, with their grandparents or another trusted sitter. When it comes to family vacations, you can avert disasters by giving thought to what the kids would also enjoy, what limitations you'll have due to their ages, and what will actually feel like a vacation for you. Do you want a mental relaxation, cultural stimulation, athletic exertion, adventure, service, sun and fun on a beach, mountains with fresh air and hiking, a photography trip to Europe, or a week in the mountains with your extended family? As always, a meditation is the perfect way to probe your psyche for answers. Your only goal is to identify what *you* need (rather than doing what you always do) and what will ultimately make everyone happier.

Listen to Your Intuition Meditation

1. Come to your sacred space (surely you have one by now!) or some place that is soothing in your home.
2. Sit cross-legged on a folded blanket.
3. Make sure that your spine is lengthened.
4. Before you begin your meditation practice, it is nice to set an intention. (An intention can be thought of as a prayer.) Maybe your intention would be to take your family on a vacation with peace in your heart and peace with all the relationships in the family. It doesn't matter what you do when everyone is feeling peace within their hearts. The vacation will be amazing.
5. After you formulate your intention, close your eyes, and relax your jaw by parting your teeth. Only your lips will be touching.
6. Bring your hands, palms facing upward, onto your knees. (This hand gesture is with the intention of receiving wisdom from the universe—or from God, if you prefer.)
7. Anchor your breath to a phrase, such as something from your intention.
8. Inhale. *May I have peace within my heart.*
9. Exhale. *May my family have peace within their hearts.*
10. As you breathe, keep repeating your intention.
11. Try this for as long as twenty minutes if you are able. Set a kitchen timer or your cell phone alarm so you won't be distracted with watching a clock.
12. After the timer goes off, sit in stillness, recognizing that an intention is powerful and that you can have faith and trust in the process. Notice how calm you feel, and savor this moment!

When you are able to keep your thoughts in stillness for a few minutes, you will know what to do. The intuition you have just awakened will guide you.

VACATION EXPECTATIONS

*"How beautiful to do nothing and
then rest afterward."*

—SPANISH PROVERB

Unless your family never took real vacations when you were a child, you probably enjoyed trips that turned into adventures. Maybe you got to travel to exotic locations, like Hawaii, Bali, or Europe; maybe your family alternated between renting beach cottages and mountain retreats; maybe your vacations centered around sports, like skiing in the winter and biking tours in the summer; or maybe your family considered vacation an opportunity to drive long distances to visit relatives. No matter what, you likely found adventure in each experience. Children are notorious for complaining while the vacation is occurring and later raving about how much fun they had when they tell their friends all about it. Thus, you likely have memories that represent *vacation* to you, which can be swell if the vacations you take now measure up, but not so good if the vacations you take now fall short.

One of the best things you can do to guarantee that your family vacation will go well is to manage your expectations. Romanticizing, or envisioning luxury beyond what your budget can afford, may lead to disappointment. One of the best ways to guarantee that your expectations are reasonable is to get clear on what you want to have happen—and to have your husband and children do the same.

As mom, you need to decide what you want to create by taking a family vacation; what outcome is your greatest priority? Is it closeness, fun, bonding, adventurous exploration, or laid-back relaxation? What do you *need* from your vacation, and what does your family need?

Do another inner child meditation (described in Chapter 7) to explore what worked for you as a child, when and if you went on vacation.

1. Lie down someplace really comfortable. You can lie in a tub of warm water if that is what will "float your memory boat."

2. Close your eyes, and think back to when you were a child. Think about your favorite childhood experience (even if it wasn't a vacation). Think about those times when you were happiest as a child. What were you doing? Who was with you? How did you look, and what were you wearing?

3. See if you are able to look at the child (who was you) from the outside, as though you could look down and see yourself as a child.

4. Bring back a happy memory from a childhood vacation, even if it is a few moments.

   Know that you cannot recreate an experience but you may generate a feeling that will guide you in what you want from your upcoming family vacation.

5. Linger with these sensations and feelings until you feel refreshed.

Jot down any memories or ideas, and if you have siblings, call them to talk about your childhood and happy memories. If your parents are available, call them as well and talk to them about happy vacation memories, or just happy times.

This should all help you bring a joyful, childlike quality to planning your family vacation. Think about each of the immediate family members. What would bring joy and peace to them as well as to you?

After the visualizing exercise and talking with your extended family and your immediate family, you may be quite clear that driving an RV across the country is not your cup of vacation tea, after all. With the help of your family, you may consciously (and gleefully) choose to find a quaint cottage, located on a lake or pond in a nearby area.

Me-Time: Make Yourself a Priority

Even vacationing moms can feel frazzled, so no matter what kind of vacation you plan, always add a little extra me-time. Regardless of where you go, you can find a spa and get a massage, or wander off alone to explore antique shops, or visit galleries, or find a babysitter so you and your husband can have a romantic dinner in an expensive restaurant. When you make your plans, explore options for your me-time so you'll have something extra special to look forward to—and calendar it into your plans.

DESTINATION DETOX

"Spiritual progress is like detoxification.
Things have to come up in order to be released.
Once we have asked to be healed, then our
unhealed places are forced to the surface."

—MARIANNE WILLIAMSON

Once you've arrived at your vacation destination, one of the first orders of business is to detox. That's right, you need a meditation to clear your mind and ready yourself for a fun-filled vacation. You want to shed the worries that drag you down; you want to lighten up your spirit and open your mind and your heart to more fully experience what's ahead. Whether you're aware of it or not, you can hold a lot of negative feelings and memories in your cells, which means all those bad times are along for the ride. The beginning of a vacation is a great time to shed some unwelcome baggage and open your body and soul to new experiences.

Releasing Tension Meditation

1. Bring yourself to a comfortable seated posture on the floor with a folded blanket or towel to sit on.
2. Breathe in for the count of five, and exhale for the count of seven.
3. Breathe in for the count of five, and exhale for the count of seven.

4. Stay with this breath until you are feeling calm (or at least calmer than before).

5. Have the intention of letting some things go.

6. Your breath is creating space. You are not able to bring new things into your life until you let some things go.

7. With your eyes closed, notice how you are feeling in your physical body. Notice if you feel tension in your shoulders. Do you hold the weight of the world on your shoulders? Most moms carry more than their share of worries.

8. With your eyes closed, think about who or what is on your shoulders, causing you to feel weighted down.

9. You may have your entire family lined up on your shoulders. Picture all of them lined up. What else or who else is there? Friends, aging parents, work responsibilities? Take time to really notice all of the people and "stuff" you are carrying.

10. Inhale into your belly.

11. Exhale slowly; as you lean to your right, reach your right arm straight out and tilt over until your fingertips touch the floor.

12. Watch as everything and everyone slides off your shoulders, joyfully "listening" as they scream "Wheeeee" while soaring down the slide that is your arm. Let them slide off, trusting that they will be fine, that they don't need to rest on your shoulders (and that you don't need them to rest there either!).

13. Inhale into your belly.

14. Exhale slowly, and repeat the same motion with your left arm, letting everything and everyone on that side slide off. You may have to shake your arm, as some people will (consciously or unconsciously) hold on really tight, even if everyone (especially you) knows it's good to let them go.

15. You have created space with your exhale being longer than your inhale. You have also let quite a few things go. You can now fill up with calm, peace, joy, or whatever it is that you need.

16. When you fully exhale, you have given all that you can. There is nothing more than to have faith in your next inhale.

You now have a vacation happening in your shoulders, and the fun has just begun!

Yoga to the Rescue!

If you arrive at your destination with jetlag or car fatigue, yoga poses will replenish your energy and get you off to a good start. Legs up the wall (see Chapter 6) or downward-facing dog (see Chapter 3) will do wonders, but there are a few more you can try as well. Remember that yoga poses shouldn't hurt, and they don't have to be perfectly executed. They are methods of stretching (and breathing while stretching) that limber up your muscles, release tension, and reunite your physical, mental, and spiritual bodies. Yoga is a physical meditation that you can bolster with affirmations.

Seated Forward Bend

Sit down on the floor, with your legs extended. (Sit on a towel if you're in a hotel and not sure how clean the carpet is.) Inhale, and as you exhale, reach your hands toward your feet, hinging at the hips. Relax your arms by your legs, and stay folded over, with your head and neck relaxed. Forward-bending postures will calm the nerves while also stretching leg and spine muscles.

Now your lower back is on vacation!

Simple Stretch

1. Lie down on the floor on your back; put a towel down if you're in a hotel and not sure how clean the carpet is.
2. Bend your knees, and bring the soles of your feet to the floor. Your arms are by your sides.
3. Inhale, reaching your arms up and over your head, resting them, palm sides up, on the floor above your head.
4. Exhale, bringing your knees toward your chest.
5. Inhale, reaching your feet up toward the ceiling and flexing your feet (toes toward your forehead).
6. Exhale, bringing your knees back toward your chest.
7. Inhale, bringing the soles of your feet back to the floor, using your abdominal muscles to control the movement.
8. Exhale, bringing your arms back to the floor beside you.
9. Inhale, lifting your hips upward a few inches.
10. Exhale, bringing your hips back down.
11. Repeat this simple stretch as many times as you would like.

Now your entire body is gearing up for fun! Bring on the vacation!

CROSSED WIRES AND ROAD BUMPS

*"Life is like an ever-shifting kaleidoscope—a
slight change, and all patterns alter."*

—SHARON SALZBERG

All vacations hit road bumps—times when kids are cranky, exhausted, whiney, uncooperative, and homesick. Of course, moms (and dads) can also be all of those things, and more. Most of the time you'll see warning signs, and when you do, it's smart to nip it in the bud. Just stop whatever you're doing, and handle the situation. If your children are hungry, feed them. If your smaller children are too tired to behave well, take them back to your hotel room and put them down for a nap. If they're angry, sort out the situation, reaching a compromise, if possible. If it's all of the above, maybe everyone needs a cooling-off period.

Hugging Meditation

For small children, lie together on a bed, wrap your arms around them, and tell them you're going to take a nap together. Recreate a very soft "ocean breath" by breathing through your nose and making the sound of "Haaaaa." Tell them that mother dogs will exhale through their nose with a full breath like this to calm their puppies, and that when the puppies hear this breath, they know it is time to settle down. Have them join in as you all breathe like the ocean (or a mamma dog soothing her puppies), and they will calm down in minutes. You can then use this same technique in other stressful situations.

For older kids, wrap your arms around them and pull them in for an embracing, firm hug. Envision your two hearts melding. This will be good for the both of you. Hug dad, too.

Home Sweet Home

When some are suffering from a bout of homesickness, doing something that reminds them of home can feel very comforting. Maybe it's going out for pizza, going to a movie together, staying in to watch a DVD together, reading the children their favorite bedtime stories, or even going to church. Anything that feels like home is likely to help you through the rough patch so you can resume enjoying your vacation.

Vacation Overload

Often on vacations children can become overstimulated. Children like routine, so being away from home is harder on them. They may also feel bombarded by new situations, new people, new food, new everything. Even older children can feel overstimulated, although they may have the advantage of being able to recognize how they feel and why they feel that way. Younger children, however, may require a mom's radar to figure out when enough is enough and the child needs quiet, reassurance, or other special coddling.

Mirror Me Meditation

Sit cross-legged on the floor, with your child facing you. Have your knees lightly touching. Have both of you bring your hands up, and hold your hands about a half inch away from your child's. Tell your child that you're going to move your hands in circles really slowly and that his task is to mirror your motions. Start off slowly and simply, but expand the circles and add some wackiness to make it fun. Before you know it, you will both be collapsing with laughter. Take turns being the mirror, encouraging all kinds of shapes and swirls to see if you can keep up with each other. It works because mirroring takes concentration and will calm frayed nerves—and it's just a whole lot of fun!

Mindful Mom

When a child is overstimulated, it's the perfect time for mom to spend a few minutes completely focused on the child and his needs. Often all a child needs is reassurance that she is safe, that you are paying attention to her needs, that her needs matter, and that you are eager to do whatever you can do—within reason—to help her feel more comfortable and to make her vacation the fun experience that you intended it to be. Even older children may benefit from a few quiet moments alone with mom.

As always, connect by looking into their eyes, listening closely to what they're saying aloud (and underneath the words), and by gently touching them. Sometimes an arm and hand massage, a neck massage, or a heartfelt hug can do wonders.

Vacation Venom

It's also a given that arguments will occur. Someone's going to snap at someone else, and any pent-up feelings or low-level anxiety can explode, leading to petty arguments, squabbling, and hurt feelings. If your family is on the brink, there are yoga poses you can do that will soothe feelings, smooth over disappointments, calm the situations, and renew bonds.

Ostrich Pose

The pose is called *ostrich* because ostriches sleep with their heads buried in the sand.

Stand with your backs toward each other, with your feet apart. If there are more than two of you, stand in a circle with backs toward the center. Inhale together, and reach your hands up toward the ceiling. Exhale, and fold forward, hands touching or reaching toward the floor underneath you. Stay folded over, and look at each other. You can make silly faces at each other. Any time that you can share smiles and laughter, the tension will lighten.

Half Moon Pose

1. Face each other, standing really tall. If there are more than two of you, stand in a circle facing in.
2. Reach your arms up as high as you are able.
3. Reach over to one side. If mom goes to her right then the child will go to his left, so that your body looks like a half moon.
4. Straighten, and then reach over to the other side with both arms.
5. Keep bending right, then left, until you feel ready to move on.

Frog Pose

This is a fun pose and really good for your lower back.

1. Face each other.
2. Stand with your feet slightly more than hip-width apart.
3. Squat down, trying to keep your heels pressing downward. If it's too stressful on your hamstrings, raise your ankles to a comfortable position.
4. Once you are comfortable in the frog pose, reach out and hold hands with the person you are facing.
5. You can even slowly lean back a little bit, being careful not to pull the lighter child forward.
6. Stay for a few breaths. After you let go, you both can frog hop about the room, making frog sounds.

Give Everyone a Day

Often disagreements occur because someone feels left out or disappointed. To make each person feel equally important, and to teach your children to embrace a cooperative spirit, try giving each person a day on which they decide what the family does. Smaller children might opt for an amusement park; older children might want to go to a movie or to a concert; parents might opt for a walking tour of a historic district—and everyone might groan at what they're being asked to endure. Still, all have to step up and be team players, cooperatively honoring each family member's choice. If everyone stays cheerful, it makes one and all feel important and closer to each other.

MEDITATION SPLENDOR

"To sit in the shade on a fine day and look upon the verdant green hills is the most perfect refreshment."

—JANE AUSTEN

The best part about vacations that involve being in nature is that they offer incredible opportunities to meditate. Because you're more relaxed on vacation and likely in an unfamiliar environment, appreciating the nature around you is a marvelous way to deepen your experience. Following are ideas for meditations that will bring another level of experience to your vacation setting.

Water Meditation I

If you are near a river, a lake, or the ocean, water meditations are an ideal way to feel at one with your surroundings. We are, after all, up to 75 percent water!

Lie down on your bed, and consider your relationship with water. Our bodies are mostly water. The chemistry of the water in our bodies is like the chemistry of the salt water in the ocean. Do you feel the pull of the moon like the tides?

Water Meditation II

Walk around and see if you can feel watery. Move as if you had no bones. Feel fluid. Walk to a place to lie down. Close your eyes. Consider the healing properties of water, washing away all your concerns:

- Rivers of tears, sometimes pouring out of you, and at other times, just a trickle. Salty tears.
- Tributaries of capillaries nourishing every single part of your body. The flowing blood in your veins and arteries bringing oxygen to every part of your body.
- All the systems of your body . . . flowing.

Water Meditation III

Imagine you are on a sailboat. Are you able to let your sails down? Can you enjoy your journey through the waters of life? Or are you always trying to control the outcome? Let your thoughts come and go without judgment.

Mountain Meditation I

Being in the mountains is also a unique experience. The clear air, fresh breezes, sweeping vistas, and abundant foliage all provide soul nourishment.

1. Lie down outside, if possible; if not, lie down on a bed.
2. Close your eyes.

3. Breathe long, slow breaths.
4. Let your entire body surrender into the support of the earth.
5. Picture Mother Earth wrapping her arms around you with healing love.
6. Feel the gentle mountain breeze blow across your face and your body.
7. Feel the coolness.

Stand up slowly, and take a refreshing breath, drawing in the fresh mountain air.

Mountain Meditation II

1. Lie down if possible; if not, sit comfortably.
2. Imagine you are lying in the middle of a mountain meadow filled with wildflowers. Smell the earth, the fragrant flowers, the wild grasses. Feel the warm sun on your body. Listen to the sounds of birds in the distance, the humming of insects, the sound of the breeze rustling the trees.
3. Imagine that a mountain stream is off in the distance, and you can hear the movement of water.
4. Imagine all of your concerns, worries, hurts, and disappointments flowing down the stream like fallen leaves. Imagine them floating away.
5. Each time a thought comes into your mind, let it flow down the stream. Let it go.
6. Become so still that all of your senses are alive.
7. Listen to the quiet sound of a fawn chewing young, green, wild grasses.

8. Relax, and let go of all thought.
9. Come to a place of peace, quiet, healing.

When you feel calm at your center, stand up slowly, and take a short walk in your surroundings, reveling in the beauty around you.

Culture Meditation

If you've traveled to an exotic location, a foreign country, or some place foreign to you—such as a city if you live in the country, and vice versa—opening your eyes, your mind, and your heart to the experience can take you to a whole new level. Often all you need is to ground yourself in who you are and how you feel about people, no matter where your physical body has landed.

Shine Your Light Meditation
1. Sit in a comfortable seated pose, cross-legged if you are able. Or sit on a chair with your feet flat on the ground.
2. Bring your hands together, and vigorously rub them until you feel lots of heat.
3. Bring your heated hands over your heart center. Your heart center is in the center of your sternum, over your heart. Put one hand over the other.
4. Imagine the heat going into your heart and lighting a candle. (Consider that when you go into a very dark room, just one candle can bring light.)
5. Bring all of your awareness to the heat and light at your heart center.

6. Consider this heat and light to be all the love that you have.

7. Send beams of this light/love in the direction of your family, first to your children and your husband or partner. As you send love, your heart becomes bigger and bigger and brighter with love and light.

8. Send beams of light to other family and friends, and to your colleagues. Send more light and love to neighbors, even those whom you do not necessarily like . . . send them more light and love.

9. Next, send love and light to those whom you may see day-to-day but do not really know: the barista who makes your coffee every morning at the coffee shop, your mail deliverer, the school crossing guard. Send them your light and love.

10. Let this light in your heart become a giant ball of love and energy.

11. Send this giant ball of light and love to your community, to your town, state, country. Send this love and light to all of the corners of the earth. Know that your love is boundless, without borders or prejudice.

Weather Meditation

Weather is always thwarting vacation plans. Just when you're headed out the door for a bike ride, a thunderstorm comes driving across the lake. You're at the ski resort, and there's no snow; or you're at the beach, and it's cloudy and cold. Particularly with children, enduring weather can either be an adventure or a mishap. Fortunately, meditation can lift your spirits and help you help everyone else enjoy the experience, whether or not the weather cooperates. We cannot predict or control the weather—or for that matter, anything else—but we can feel a change in the air and learn how to feel more comfortable with unpredictability.

Meditation on How to Expect the Unexpected

When you get upset or anxious about something unexpected (like the weather), you have already lost sight of living in the moment. As you become more anxious, focus on slowing and calming your mind.

1. Sit or lie down.
2. Tune in to your breath. Your breath brings you back to the present moment.
3. Notice the quality of the breath: how it is cool as you inhale and warm as you exhale.
4. Notice the feeling under your nostrils as the breath moves in and out.
5. Take a moment as you are focusing on your breath to notice how you are feeling. Disappointed? Anxious?
6. Do a body scan, from the top of your head to your toes.
7. Say each body part as you scan, and notice any sensations.
8. Notice if you have tightness in any parts of your body. Are you gripping in your body? Loosen your grip. Do you feel like you are losing control when the weather (or anything unexpected) changes your plans? Surrender your desire to control.
9. Notice your emotions. It is easy to have joy when everything is going the way you want. When it is always sunny on a summer vacation, it is easy to smile and be lighthearted. It is much more challenging when things do not work according to plans.

10. Change can be uncomfortable. Notice where you feel it in your body . . . physically, emotionally, or mentally. When have you felt like this before? Take some time with this. Go back and remember when your body felt this way before.
11. Notice and bring yourself back to the present moment, to your breath.

Change is hard and can cause you to feel all kinds of emotions. Meditation can bring a sense of ease. No matter what happens with vacation plans, you can always bring your focus to your inner body. You can choose to still your thoughts. You can choose to go to the place of wisdom within. See what it has to say. The more you can calm yourself with focus on breath and on moment-to-moment experience, the clearer your intuition will be.

Family Meditation

If you're visiting relatives on vacation, take advantage of the opportunity to reconnect on deeper levels and strengthen those family bonds. One way to accomplish coming together is to cook a meal together, one where everyone pitches in.

Mindful Meal Meditation

Slowing down the cooking and sharing of meals can be a marvelous mindfulness meditation. All you have to do is have each and every person participate in some way, whether it's planning, shopping, cooking, setting the table, selecting the music, preparing drinks, making the homemade ice cream, cleaning, or entertaining.

There's a job for everyone, and working together will be much more fun than having a few people slave alone in the kitchen.

Being mindful of your contribution, enjoying the feelings that arise in loving and supporting your family, and being mindful of the strong bonds that connect you, will bring everyone joyfully together.

When it is time to eat, invite everyone to gather around the table, join hands, and close their eyes. Offer thanks that you are all together, enjoying each other's company, nurturing and supporting and loving each and every person. After the food has been passed around, invite everyone to open up and to share what they appreciate about each other, the family, those who are not with you anymore. During the meal, tell stories about family, childhood, where your ancestors were from. Tell the stories that make everyone laugh, like when your great-grandfather ran away from home when he was nine, in nothing but his underwear. Tell stories about how your great-grandmother used to bake the thinnest, most delicious tea cookies and the tastiest lemon meringue pie. Talk about how your mother used to dance in her bare feet in her kitchen as she cooked.

Before dessert, bring out the camera, and snap pictures of everyone around the table. After the meal put on music that you and your siblings loved as teenagers, turn it up, and dance as you all pitch in to clean the table, do the dishes—all while talking, laughing, and dancing together.

After dinner, play games together.

HOME AGAIN, HOME AGAIN

"The very last (lojong, 'mind training') slogan is 'Train wholeheartedly.' You could say 'Live wholeheartedly.' Let everything stop your mind and let everything open your heart. And you could say, 'Die wholeheartedly, moment after moment.' Moment after moment, let yourself die wholeheartedly."

—PEMA CHÖDRÖN

Vacation is over, and you've just pulled into your driveway. The kids have been dozing in their car seats, and you're barely awake yourself. Once you get the kids and the luggage inside, all you want to do is collapse into your bed. We say, go for it . . . and get a good night's sleep.

The next morning, however, you need to get everyone's body, mind, and soul grounded. Yes, you want to treasure the memories and share stories for weeks afterward, but you also need to settle back in, resuming life as you know it—only better. Here's a short meditation to welcome you home and to close the book . . . as our journey together is now complete.

Thankfulness Meditation

Sit quietly, close your eyes, and concentrate on one thing that you are truly thankful for right now. Hold this image in your mind, appreciating all the aspects that make you feel such gratitude and pleasure. Allow the feeling of gratitude for your many blessings to warm your heart. Breathe in and out slowly, quietly, enjoying the stillness of hearth and home. When you are ready, ask your higher power (God, the divine, the creative spirit, or whatever spiritual reference holds meaning for you) to "Help me open my heart to a fuller understanding of myself and of my family. Give me the grace to walk on my own path to new growth. Amen."

CHAPTER SUMMARY

This chapter had a wealth of meditations that could truly help you weather any vacation crises, and there are always low points and high points during vacations. Let's review what you've learned:

- The hardest part is getting on the road, and the best way to do that is to forget about counting your blessings and focus on counting your breaths instead.
- Before you plan your next vacation, spending time to meditate on what *you* need from your vacation will help you create one that feels more satisfying. Tapping into your intuition helps a whole bunch.
- Fantasy is fine, but managing expectations will help everyone enjoy the experience for what it is, rather than feeling disappointed by what it isn't.
- Upon arrival, taking time for a detoxifying meditation will smooth over any residual frustration and set the stage for fun. Downward-facing dog rocks!

- Even if it's heaven on earth, everyone will occasionally miss home. Being a mindful mom and giving each child what you already know will evoke happy memories of home will cure the problem and allow everyone to resume having fun.
- Yoga poses are a fabulous way to bring everyone together and resolve petty arguments or building frustration. Some will have everyone rolling with laughter, which is exactly what the vacation doctor ordered.
- Meditations that include appreciation for the beauty around you will deepen your vacation experience.
- Vacations that include visiting extended families offer rare opportunities to bond through meditation and storytelling.

We've thoroughly enjoyed sharing what we've learned in our journeys as mothers, and we hope you'll fall in love with meditation, with yoga, with life, and most of all with yourself as a mother. Don't forget that you can use the guided meditations on the CD to deepen your meditations and to develop a meditation practice, something we highly encourage!

Meanwhile, peace be with you, and with those you love. Namaste!

APPENDIX A

Getting Started with Meditation

The key to starting a meditation practice that you will look forward to is to think of meditation as the creation of your own oasis, a place where you will refresh yourself. In the beginning, you will want to select a place where you can begin your meditation practice and continue at your pace, in your own style, without distraction. Ideally this would be a dedicated room or garden for meditation. See Chapter 1 for more information on creating a sacred space for your meditation.

If you can't dedicate an entire room, try to avoid placing a shrine in a closet or bathroom, because this subconsciously marginalizes your practice. It would be better to partition part of a main room with a screen or furniture. If your meditation space will be located outside, make sure you have a comfortable chair, bench, or cushion, and avoid extremes of heat and cold.

Obviously, a place where interference is at a minimum is ideal. You should find a space where the telephone can be turned off and sounds from other rooms can be shut out.

Electronic and electrical equipment can also be a nuisance. The continual hum of a computer fan or the low buzz of a fluorescent light will be distracting when you are starting to focus your attention inward. Make sure you can easily shut down these machines without jeopardizing your safety or comfort.

REMOVING DISTRACTIONS

A cluttered space is a distraction. Piles of unopened mail and grocery receipts have their own hypnotic power that you may need to escape. An orderly, clean environment encourages the feeling of readiness and ease.

Most of all, your meditation space should not be a place where foot traffic will disrupt your focus. An area where others will be eating, ironing, or watching television isn't a good choice. Members of your household should not be passing through your space. This will be your sanctuary, so it should offer peace and privacy from the outside world.

Of course, you have to work with the space that you have, and most of us are not lucky enough to have an ideal space to meditate. Complete elimination of distraction is neither possible nor desirable, because the annoying elements in our spaces become grist for the mill of meditation. Behind every distraction is some attachment waiting to be uncovered and diffused, some adjustment in attitude that needs to be made. So strive to have a clean, orderly, inspiring, out-of-the-way place to meditate, but realize that this will never be entirely the case.

FINDING THE RIGHT ACCESSORIES

The meditation environment can reflect your personal tastes and your goals. You can experiment with this, choosing those elements that suit your personality and home décor. In Chapter 1, we talk about creating an altar for your space.

Comfort is an important concern. You may be spending some time in this space, and you don't want to be discouraged if it feels uncomfortable. You should be able to maintain a comfortable temperature, and keep a warm blanket or throw nearby in case it gets drafty.

The wall space that surrounds you is another consideration. You may want a blank canvas for your initial meditation practice, or you may feel more at ease with the usual décor. Then again, you may want to choose special wall hangings, a set of favorite prints or a painting. Many meditators pay great attention to such details in their meditation room, but keep in mind that your approach may change.

Lighting is another point that you want to resolve. Whether you have access to a lot of natural light or depend on artificial sources, make sure it can be adjusted to minimum and maximum levels. Candles are often used for focus in meditation, but they pose safety problems if not supported securely. Likewise, incense should be burned in containers that will catch the ashes.

Plants and flowers are other additions to the meditation space that can lend a connection to nature and create a fresh atmosphere. You can even use plants as visual reminders of your meditation practice. Each time you water the plants, you will be reminded that you will also need the refreshment of a meditation session. And as the plant grows, so will your proficiency in personal growth and self-awareness.

Music is a big consideration for the beginner. You may want to incorporate background music to get in the mood for meditation, or it may be necessary to balance outside, distracting noises in the dwelling or the street. You can also find useful training tapes and inspirational recordings that are preliminary tools for meditation.

SITTING POSITIONS

First and most importantly, allow your spine to be upright and immobile. This position allows for optimum breathing and less strain on the body overall for maintaining one position over an extended period. Nothing should interfere with circulation. Besides a practice of proper breathing to aid circulation, the right posture ensures that the entire body can oxygenate without hindrance.

For the spine to be upright, you will be either sitting or standing for meditation practice. Sitting postures require a firm foundation, but at the same time, enough padding should be under you to promote circulation and comfort. Keep in mind that circulation is more important than how your position looks. You can sit on the floor or in a chair, but if you choose a chair, be sure your feet are supported—either by the floor, a footrest, or a cushion.

Wear comfortable, loose-fitting clothing for meditation. When you have found a style or tradition that is likely to "stick," consider investing in garments and tools appropriate to the particular tradition and level of initiation. While clothes and accessories will not buy spiritual insight, they do help to set the tone for the meditation session and should not be disregarded.

Try sitting in several different positions. If, within five minutes, you start to feel numbness in your feet, legs, knees, or bottom, get up and move about for another five minutes. Then try another sitting position. Do this until you find a position that doesn't impose any restrictions or discomfort for at least fifteen minutes at a time.

Here are some additional thoughts about sitting:

- If you choose to sit in a chair, make sure you have a sturdy but comfortable sitting chair with a tall back that will keep your spine straight and your back supported.
- Keep your feet flat on the floor and lean back to rest your neck if necessary.
- Avoid tight clothing or footwear, furniture that pushes against your limbs, and slippery fabric covers that will interfere with comfort and relaxation.
- If you choose to be seated on the floor, make sure the surface is completely flat, using a rug or pad on hard surfaces, followed by a seat cushion or bench that fits you while seated.
- Choose a posture that allows you to place your knees as close to the floor as possible so that your spine will remain upright in a beneficial position.
- If your back tires easily, you can lean against a wall with your legs stretched out in front of you.

For sitting meditation, the lotus posture is viewed as the ideal way to connect the body with the vital energy of earth. Like a lotus, your trunk is akin to the flower's root, grounding itself to the stabilizing force of the land. At the same time, the watery regions of thought and emotion surround you, yet the meditation process enables you to float through them unaffected.

STANDING MEDITATION

You may find yourself at a time or place where traditional sitting meditation is not possible. If that should be the case, standing meditation is quite effective, although it may not be comfortable for extended periods. Any meditation lasting less than fifteen minutes is adaptable to standing meditation.

Stand with your spine upright and your shoulders straight. This isn't a military stance, because that would be tiring. Instead, your shoulders should be evenly balanced on both sides. Your chin is tilted slightly upward but not stretched. Stand with your feet about twelve inches apart, far enough to balance your weight evenly. Your hands may be placed with palms against your thighs. Or you may find it more comfortable to hold both hands close to the center of your body, palms inward. Do not cross or fold your arms.

PRONE MEDITATION

Prone meditation is also called lying meditation and in yoga, *Savasana*, or the corpse. Despite the eerie name, this posture makes it possible to maintain mental and physical stillness while lying down.

Start by choosing a firm surface. If you're on the floor, make sure it is padded enough not to press against portions of the body and cause numbness. If the surface is too comfortable, such as a mattress, it may encourage lethargy and sleep. Try to find a happy medium.

Lie flat on your back, with your spine touching as much of the floor surface as possible. Relax your neck and shoulders, and allow your arms to relax with open palms about six inches away from your body. Look directly up without stretching your neck in any way. If the light from the ceiling is too strong, use a floor lamp instead.

FINDING THE RIGHT TIME TO MEDITATE

When is a good time for meditation? The diurnal (daily) clock is the one we set our conscious life to, but few are aware of the subtle forces at work each day. At sunrise, the environment is illuminated and natural life awakens. Depending on the time of year and geographic location, the sun may begin to warm the earth, and the temperature arouses certain animal species to either come out into the light or retreat. At noon, the sun is directly overhead, with light and heat at their most intense. Midday is a vital time, and the life force is at its peak. At sunset, the light diminishes as it sinks below the horizon and most active life begins to withdraw. The midnight hour is also a pivotal time of the day, although few are awake to appreciate it.

These four periods are regarded as the "peak points" of the day, the diurnal rhythm. The sun is either on one of the horizons (east or west), the midheaven (at noon), or the nadir (at midnight). This is how it is viewed both astronomically and in astrology, although each has a different perspective on the meaning. But both agree that these peak points are the vital times of the day and influence human behavior in profound ways.

So when should you meditate? Actually, the peak points of the day are when you are most ambitious and may want to practice, but these times often conflict with other duties.

Many people find it most useful to start the day with a morning meditation. By clearing the mind and consciously experiencing stillness, the day does not seem so daunting or ordinary—whichever the case may be. An early evening meditation similarly stills and clears the mind of the day's events.

Whatever time you find best fits your schedule, try to keep it away from mealtimes. If you have not eaten for several hours, a growling stomach may interrupt your meditation session. And if you're meditating right after a meal, the digestive process could similarly be disruptive. Besides, sitting for an extended period right after eating tends to compress the esophagus, bringing on acid reflux or heartburn.

KNOWING HOW LONG TO MEDITATE

How long each meditation section should take depends on how much time you have available! Even just a few minutes can make a difference. However, the longer you are able to meditate, the more benefits you will experience from the process.

Setting a timer or placing a clock in your meditation space may be useful in the beginning, but you don't want the clock to rule your session. In fact, the passage of time is always monitored by the subconscious mind. In meditation, this awareness often comes forward. So, set yourself up mentally for a a specific length of time, such as five minutes, and stop when you think you've achieved it. If not, try it again the next time you have a session. Since meditation is a process of becoming aware, the passage of time will make itself known soon enough. Remember, you are leaving the world of schedules and moving into the timeless.

After a while you will find yourself able to meditate at any time and, eventually, any place. Remember that this is only a commitment to yourself, and not to any one person or long-term goal. It's a gift of time that you are investing in your well-being.

Index

A

After-school hours, 55–72
  extracurricular activities, 67–70
  homework strategies, 64–65
  me-time during, 63, 69–71
  rebalancing meditation, 56–58
  spiritual development, 58–60
  yoga meditations, 58–62
Alther, Lisa, 25
Angelou, Maya, 30, 47, 63
Animal yoga, 61–62
Anticipation, 49
Anxiety, 142–43
Appreciating others, 81–82
Art and Science of Mindfulness, 14
Austen, Jane, 185
Awakening meditation, 8–9

B

Back bend, 151–52
Bailey, Pearl, 74
Balanced, staying, 87–88
Bath-time rituals, 101–2
Beckham, Victoria, 76
Bedtime hours, 91–109
  off-nights, 98–100
  rituals for, 92–97, 101–6
  yoga poses for, 94–97
Bedtime meditations, 93–97
Bedtime rituals, 92–97, 101–6
Bedtime yoga, 94–96

Bender, Sierra, 113
Bombeck, Erma, 86
Bottome, Phyllis, 136
Breath, catching, 63
Breathing exercises
  counting to ten, 26
  description of, 5–7
  for energy, 23–24, 34–36, 52–53,
    144–45
  for relaxation, 5–7, 31, 35–36, 72,
    131–32, 140, 169
Breath, of joy, 144–45
Breath, watching, 131–32
Brontë, Charlotte, 92
Brown, Rita Mae, 135
Buck, Pearl S., 5
Buddha, 137
Buddhists, 7, 13–14, 20, 22
Busy mornings, 3–31. *See also* Morning meditations

C

Catching breath, 63
Chakras
  description of, 7
  heart chakra, 16
  second chakra, 158–59
  third-eye chakra, 67–68, 118–19
  throat chakra, 9–10
Chattering mind, 50–51, 59, 65, 129
Chauffer mom, 25–28

Child's pose, 95–96
Chödrön, Pema, 8, 19, 33, 107, 131, 153, 193
Churchill, Jill, 3
Cobbler's pose, 96
Cobra pose, 35–39
Conflicts, handling, 136–38
Cooking meditation, 77–78
Corpse pose, 40–41
Couch pose, 163–64
Counting to ten, 26
Crane pose with goldfish, 60–61, 65–66
Creativity, 7, 155, 158–60
Culture meditation, 188–89

D
Daily clock, 202
Decluttering mind, 19
Decluttering space, 197
Detoxification, 176, 194
Dickinson, Emily, 143
Digestion exercises, 83–85
Digestive delight, 85
Dining out, 120–24
Dinner for friends, 125–26
Dinner hours, 73–89
  cooking meditation, 77–78
  giving thanks, 80–82
  kitchen space, 74–79
  post-dinner meditations, 83–85
  preparing meals, 74–79
Diurnal rhythm, 202
Double-duty serenity, 130
Douzel, Catherine, 46

Dukakis, Olympia, 104

E
Eating slowly, 115–16
Energy cleansing shower, 70–71
Energy, flow of, 22, 24
Energy meditation, 11–12
Energy, wheels of, 7, 118, 158. See also Chakras
Entertaining, 125–26
Expectations meditation, 190–91
Extracurricular activities, 67–70
Eye-cupping meditation, 30

F
Family meditation, 191–92
Fish pose, 12–13
Folding over pose, 149
Fold over pose, 147–48
Follow your breath meditation, 169
Forward bend, 150–51
French, Marilyn, 83
Frog pose, 184

G
Gift giving, 82
Giving thanks, 74–75, 80–82
Goldberg, Natalie, 114
Grace, saying, 80–81
Graham, Martha, 34

H
Half moon pose, 183
Hanson, Judith, 141
Hara breath, 23–24

Hobbies, 153–66
  creativity, 155, 158–60
  meditative hobbies, 153–57
  time for, 67–70, 140
Homework strategies, 64–65
Hugging meditation, 180–81
Hug knees posture, 152–53

I
Inner child, honoring, 160–62
In-out meditation, 105
Intentions, 5, 8–10, 50–51, 81, 119–
  20, 133. *See also* Prayers
Intuition meditations, 118–19,
  172–73

J
Joy, breath of, 144–45

K
Kenny, Elizabeth, 64
Khalsa, Gurmukh Kaur, 56
Kitchen space, 74–79
Klempner, Joan, 101

L
Lasater, Judith Hanson, 120
Last-resort meditations
  energy cleansing shower, 70–71
  energy meditations, 12–13, 51–52
  eye-cupping exercise, 30
  fish pose exercise, 12–13
  honoring inner child, 160–62
  honoring womanhood, 163–64
  legs on headboard exercise, 107–8

  phone call meditation, 88
  relaxation exercise, 66
  Shamatha with support, 131–32
  sippy straw exercise, 52
  staying balanced exercise, 87–88
  time-out break, 86–87
  watching breath exercise, 131–32
Legs on headboard exercise, 107–8
Legs on wall meditation, 127–30
Lindbergh, Anne Morrow, 167
Loren, Sophia, 42
Lotus posture, 200

M
Mantras, 27–30, 132
Meditations. *See also specific*
  meditations
  accessories for, 197–99
  for after-school, 55–72
  basics of, 5–7
  for bedtime hours, 91–109
  breathing during, 5–7
  for busy mornings, 3–31
  for dinner hours, 73–89
  expectations from, x–xii
  getting started with, 196–203
  length of, 203
  lotus posture for, 200
  for midday, 33–53
  mindfulness meditations, 2, 5,
    13–15, 46–50, 53, 151, 191–92
  positions for, 199–201
  right time for, 202–3
  sacred space for, 16–17, 196–97
  for special occasions, 111

for sports/hobbies, 135–66
for vacations, 167–95
for weekdays, 1–2
for weekends, 113–33
Meir, Golda, 49
Memories as meditation, 98–100
Me-time
  at bath-time, 101–2
  at bedtime, 97
  catching breath, 63
  for creativity, 155
  enjoying cocktails, 75
  importance of, 4
  methods for, 111
  mornings for, 19–21
  nights-off, 79
  opportunities for, 31
  pampering self, 69
  prioritizing, 175
  rituals for, 62
  sharing errands, 117
  showers, 18
  for sports/hobbies, 140
  video vacations, 45
Metta meditation, 137–38
Midday mindfulness, 33–53
  energy boosters, 34–36
  naps, 40–42
  relaxation exercise, 35–39
  tasks, 47–48
  to-do lists, 50–52
  walking, 42–44
Miller, Shannon, 146
Mind, decluttering, 19
Mindful meal meditation, 191–92

Mindful moms
  at bath-time, 92
  connecting with children, 24, 42,
    71, 124
  at naptime, 42
  playing games, 142
  reassurance from, 182, 195
  rebalancing, 58
Mindfulness
  beginning day with, 13–15, 24
  with children, 42, 42, 71, 124
  meditations for, 2, 5, 13–15,
    46–50, 53, 56–58, 68, 151,
    191–92
  practice of, 13–17
  rebalancing, 56–58
  sacred space for, 16–17
  during showers, 121–23
Mirror-me meditation, 182
Monkey Mind, 59. See also Chattering mind
Morning meditations, 3–31
  energy boosters, 11–12, 23–28
  intentions for, 8–10
  mantras, 27–30
  meditation basics, 5–7
  me-time, 19–21
  preparing for day, 13–15
  sacred space for, 16–18
Mother Teresa, 66
Mountain meditations, 186–88
Mountain pose, 60, 65–66
Mudra, 20, 21, 22, 163
Multitasking, 47–48, 147

N

Naps, 40–42, 52–53, 180

Noonan, Peggy, 40

O

Object meditation, 105–6

Ocean breath, 65, 100, 180–81

Oliver, Mary, ix

Onassis, Jacqueline Kennedy, 67

Ostrich pose, 183

P

Paltrow, Gwyneth, 11

Pelvic tilt, 159

Phone call meditation, 88

Plans, anticipating, 49

Post-dinner meditations, 83–85

Prayers, 5, 28, 81, 116, 119–20, 123–24, 172. *See also* Intentions

Q

Quinn, Sally, 125

R

Rag doll pose, 95

Rebalancing meditation, 56–58

Re-entry, 56–59

Refreshing showers, 70–71, 121–23

Releasing tension meditation, 176–78

Rewards, 117–18

Roaring lion meditation, 142–43

S

Sacred space, 16–17, 196–97

Salzberg, Sharon, 13, 50, 80, 127, 180

Savasana nap, 40–42

Saying goodnight, 96–97

Saying grace, 80–81

Schiaparelli, Elsa, 73

Scott-Maxwell, Florida, 70

Seated forward bend, 178–79

Serenity, 130

Shamatha with support, 131–32

Shapiro, Shauna L., 14

Shine-your-light meditation, 188–89

Showering me-time, 18

Showers, refreshing, 70–71, 121–23

Simple stretch, 179

Sippy straw exercise, 52

Slowing-down meditations, 114–16

Smith, Lillian, 171

Space, decluttering, 197

Special days, 111. *See also specific occasions*

Sphinx pose, 39

Spinal twist, 85

Spiritual development, 58–59

Sports, 135–66

   handling conflicts, 136–38

   sporting life, 141–43

   time for, 67–70, 140

   winners/losers, 143–45

Stillness, finding, 59

Stirring-the-pot meditation, 156–57

Straight-leg forward bend, 150–51

Sunday meditations, 127

T
Take-out meals, 79, 125
Tasks, 47–48
Tea, relaxing with, 46
Tennis ball meditation, 138–39
Tense-and-release exercise, 93–94
Tension, releasing, 176–78
Thankfulness meditation, 193–94
Thanks, giving, 74–75, 80–82
Three-part breath, 83
Throat chakra meditation, 9–10
Time-out break, 86–87
Time, stealing, 63
To-do lists, 50–51
Tree pose, 56–57, 71
Twisting pose, 148–49

U
Ujjayi breath, 65, 100. *See also* Ocean
    breath

V
Vacation overload, 181–82
Vacations, 167–95
    challenges during, 180–84
    expectations from, 173–74
    home from, 193–94
    meditation opportunities, 185–92
    "me-time" during, 175
    planning, 171–72
    reasons for, 170
    yoga during, 178–79
Vibrations, 27, 41, 119, 122
Video vacations, 45

Visualization, 49–51, 63–64, 70–71,
    75, 93, 142

W
Walking meditations, 42–44
Warrior mom, 23–24
Warrior pose, 144
Water meditations, 185–86
Weather meditation, 189–90
Weekday meditations, 1–2. *See also*
    Midday mindfulness; Morning
    meditations
Weekends, 113–33
    dining out, 120–24
    entertaining, 125–26
    intentions for, 119–20
    rewards for, 117–18
Wilcox, Ella Wheeler, 98
Williamson, Marianne, 176
Wind relieving pose, 84
Winning/losing, 143–44
Witherspoon, Reese, 55
Womanhood, honoring, 163–64

Y
Yin yoga, 146–47, 165
Yoga mat, 12, 17
Yoga poses
    for children, 58–62, 94–96
    for digestion, 83–85
    for relaxation, 6–10, 35–39
    for special occasions, 163–65
    during vacations, 178–79, 183
    yin yoga, 146–47, 165

About the Authors

Kim Dwyer, the mother of four children, has been practicing yoga for more than fifteen years and teaching yoga for more than seven years. She is a certified Phoenix Rising Yoga Therapy practitioner, who completed an intensive, 650-hour training that included traditional psychotherapy (therapeutic dialog) and body/mind integrative techniques. Ms. Dwyer also has a MA in psychology and often offers workshops combining introspection, intuition, creativity, meditation, and yoga techniques designed to help participants create balance in dealing with everyday demands. She lives on Bartlett's Island in Marshfield, MA, with her husband, Joe.

Susan Reynolds, the mother of two children, has been a journalist, writer, and editor for more than twenty-five years. Recently, she coauthored *Train Your Brain to Get Happy; Train Your Brain to Get Rich;* and *Healthiest You Ever.* She has also authored *The Everything® Enneagram Book; Change Your Shoes, Change Your Life;* and coauthored *The Everything® Guide to Personal Finance for Single Mothers.* She has also edited five anthologies: *My Mom (Dad, Teacher, and Dog) Is My Hero* and *Woodstock Revisited.* Ms. Reynolds has a BA in psychology and currently writes two blogs on Psychologytoday.com. After a great deal of meditation and contemplation, Ms. Reynolds spent a year in Paris, reinventing herself. Upon return, she created Literary Cottage, a literary consulting firm based in Boston (*www .literarycottage.com*). She is also a yoga and meditation enthusiast.